T0195582

EVERYTHING'S OK

PAST TRAUMATIC STRESS DISSOLVED

TODD BERRY
and
ROB GINNIVAN

BALBOA.
PRESS

A DIVISION OF HAY HOUSE

Balboa Press books may be ordered through booksellers or by contacting:

Balboa Press
A Division of Hay House
1663 Liberty Drive
Bloomington, IN 47403
www.balboapress.com.au
1 (877) 407-4847

Because of the dynamic nature of the Internet, any web addresses or links contained in this book may have changed since publication and may no longer be valid. The views expressed in this work are solely those of the author and do not necessarily reflect the views of the publisher, and the publisher hereby disclaims any responsibility for them.

The author of this book does not dispense medical advice or prescribe the use of any technique as a form of treatment for physical, emotional, or medical problems without the advice of a physician, either directly or indirectly. The intent of the author is only to offer information of a general nature to help you in your quest for emotional and spiritual well-being. In the event you use any of the information in this book for yourself, which is your constitutional right, the author and the publisher assume no responsibility for your actions.

Photos by Annika Ginnivan
Cover design by Jackson Aguilar
Editing by Bryony Sutherland

Print information available on the last page.

ISBN: 978-1-5043-0927-1 (sc)
ISBN: 978-1-5043-0928-8 (e)

Balboa Press rev. date: 08/30/2017

About the Authors

Todd Berry first met Rob Ginnivan in early 2014 when attending a yoga class at Soldier On headquarters. From that day onwards they embarked on a journey together to improve their own lives and those of others affected by Post-Traumatic Stress Disorder (PTSD) through the power of mindful body movement, mind stillness exercises, and overall way of being. Initially, the development of the Soldier On program was intended for contemporary veterans affected by their service. In time, both authors entered the public speaking circuit, imparting their knowledge and experience for a broader community of first responders that protect and keep society safe. These include police, firefighters, paramedics, and other emergency services professionals. Agreeing to jointly be of service to members of our society living with trauma (either directly or vicariously), Todd and Rob wrote this handbook, *Everything's OK: Past Traumatic Stress Dissolved*, to give readers hope, tools, and insight in a simple and easy to understand way.

The first part of the title, *Everything's OK*, was inspired by Todd's beloved wife, Suzy, who during a dark moment of despair during Todd's life told him, "Everything will be OK". This was an awakening moment.

The second part of the title, *Past Traumatic Stress Dissolved*, is an evolution of PTSD coined by Rob, having frequently witnessed positive life transformations of reduced traumatic stress occurring due to his mindfulness and yoga teachings to those affected by their service in the community and armed forces.

Todd Berry is a contemporary veteran who served his nation on a number of deployments in the 1990s and early 2000s. Having been exposed to traumatic events on duty, Todd has managed a Post-Traumatic Stress Disorder for several years. Now in a position to help society in other ways, Todd is an author, yoga teacher, and service ambassador to Soldier On and Frontline Yoga Inc., a volunteer for Menslink, and a sought after public speaker for a broad range of organisations. He has appeared on the *60 Minutes Australia* TV program and in a number of journals discussing his journey through PTSD and his methods to effectively manage related symptoms. He is currently providing input to the International Treatment Guidelines for PTSD from a veteran's perspective. He has a Bachelor of Leadership, Graduate Diploma of Psychological Science, and a Master of Management (HRM).

Rob Ginnivan is dedicated to helping those who help others. Having studied in the presence of Eckhart Tolle, Deepak Chopra M.D, and His Holiness The

Dalai Lama, Rob leads with compassion as an author, mindfulness coach, public speaker, yoga and meditation teacher for thousands of people around the world. As a founding board member of Frontline Yoga Inc., Rob is currently building a mindfulness framework around Australia for first responder frontline guardians affected physically and psychologically – including soldiers, paramedics, police, firefighters and those traumatised by domestic violence – leveraging his mindfulness, yoga, and meditation philosophy and methodology to assist reintegration back into the community by creating freedom in the body and stillness in the mind.

Both authors decided to write this book to provide insight to those who are in contact with or are suffering from PTSD, as well as from physical injuries experienced through their professional service and any other unfortunate life experiences. Their aspiration is to encourage people to come forward and ask for assistance, or ask how they can help others suffering, in addition to applying this insight to their everyday lives.

No one deserves to suffer. Everyone is entitled to a life of peace, calm, and happiness. With an open mind and by following the guidance given in this book, we can work towards Everything being OK now, and Dissolving our Past Traumatic Stress.

Contents

Prologue

Todd: The rationale for this book is an attempt to assist others who are suffering from PTSD and to support family members of a loved one with PTSD. I am certainly no expert on the subject and let me be clear that I am not advocating that this book will be the panacea for PTSD. Professional care from clinicians such as psychiatrists, psychologists, and general practitioners should remain as one's primary source for treatment. My initial concept was to provide the reader with empirical evidence on the efficacy of treatments for PTSD, however there are a heap of books already following this rationale. My intent is therefore to share my experiences with others and hope that this handbook will educate readers about the effects of PTSD upon service personnel, the journey of recovery and an end state of managing the condition effectively.

- The term 'recovery' will be used interchangeably with 'symptom management'. Some of you will achieve a full recovery and others will be in a position where symptom management will lead them to enjoying a fulfilling life. Some will be in stages that encompass a little bit of both.

- The term 'service personnel' will be used throughout the handbook and in this context will include members of the armed forces, first responders, and border protection agencies. I also consider that it will be of benefit to first line medical practitioners, such as nurses and doctors within emergency departments.

- The term 'warrior' will be used interchangeably as well, as I feel that the aforementioned personnel are all warriors fighting an element within their respective fields. By way of example, the armed forces are fighting tyranny; law enforcement officers are fighting crime; firefighters are, of course, fighting fire; and medical personnel are fighting time, illness, and injury.

If you are like me you may have a very short attention span, and may not necessarily have the time to read an entire warrior's guide to PTSD. If that is the case, you will be pleased to note that every chapter will commence with a summary of key points, covering a 'down and dirty' introduction to the chapter. It is not a replacement of the chapter, however, as a realist I do appreciate that sometimes we need to access key information quickly. Hopefully, the summaries will provide enough information for you to read on and complete each chapter and the booklet in its entirety. Some chapters also feature Action Plans, so you can source further guidance at a glance.

I spent eighteen years in the Australian Defence Force both as a soldier and as a commissioned officer, with the majority of my service spent as an infantryman coupled with a period in special operations. I have been battling PTSD for over ten years with many small successes and failures, and quite a few obstacles along the way. Hopefully, this book can get you to your desired end state a lot quicker than my own personal journey.

Rob: There is no one magic pill to instantly cure PTSD. It is a complex brain injury that, depending on the nature and duration of the trauma experienced, can take a varying amount of time to manage and eventually overcome. As part of an overall support mechanism structure, this handbook suggests a number of methods that could be of assistance to the person living with post-traumatic stress. The information shared is based on up-to-date research, studies, and personal experience of dealing with people living with PTSD. Although this book is heavily weighted towards the natural therapies side of healing and managing the condition, it is important to note that in many cases, an integrative approach (i.e. medical practices complemented by natural therapies) may be required until such time that the person feels well enough and is advised to rely solely on natural therapies.

People living with PTSD may have a 'support crew' including a mindfulness coach, yoga teacher, nutritionist, psychologist, psychiatrist, physiotherapist, general practitioner doctor and other valuable professionals. Without question, probably the most important members of the support crew include parents, spouse/partner, children, brothers, sisters, aunties, uncles, friends and supporters in the community. *Everything's OK: Past Traumatic Stress Dissolved* is written in such a way that anyone can open the book to a random page and instantly read something that will assist in managing the PTSD condition. By keeping the book simple, easy to understand and with suggested action plans to apply on a daily basis, the reader can feel confident that there is a safe and secure pathway to follow in an attempt to dissolve post-traumatic stress.

What is PTSD?

Key points

- PTSD is caused by exposure to a traumatic event or series of events
- The symptom picture lasts for more than one month
- PTSD can affect anyone in society, not just combatants
- PTSD is a normal reaction to an abnormal event(s)

Todd: There has been a slow evolution of names and diagnoses for soldiers with Post-Traumatic

Stress Disorder (PTSD) since World War I; initially combatants were diagnosed with 'shell shock', so named as it was believed to have been a result of concussion from the impact of artillery shells. During the modern conflicts of the 20th Century the symptom picture progressed along with the change in designation, with terms such as 'battle fatigue', 'combat stress' and the more general 1950s definition of 'gross stress reaction'.

The Diagnostic and Statistical Manual of Mental Disorders (DSM) is the go-to manual for most psychiatrists, psychologists, and general practitioners when diagnosing mental health disorders. The manual is currently in its Fifth Edition and each edition is designated by Roman Numerals, such as DSM II or DSM IV. In between publishing new editions, the American Psychiatric Association has also printed Text Revisions (TR) – as an example, DSM III TR. However, the current edition is designated by numerals: DSM 5. This rationale sounds a lot like something the Army would do. This is not an attempt to teach you to suck eggs, but I feel it is important to be on the same page as our treating clinical support team. Therefore the majority of statements referenced within this chapter will be from the extant DSM 5.

Before we tackle PTSD, it is pertinent to identify what encompasses trauma from a clinical perspective. A traumatic stressor is defined within the DSM 5 as *any event (or events) that may cause or threaten death, serious injury, or sexual violence to an individual, a close family member, or a close friend*[1]. Traumatic events include, but are not limited to, *exposure to war as a combatant or civilian, threatened or actual physical assault, threatened or actual sexual violence, being kidnapped, being taken hostage, terrorist attack, torture, natural or man-made disasters, and severe motor accidents*[1]. This is only a part of the diagnostic definition, in addition there are eight criteria that incorporate the symptom picture and lead to a formal diagnosis. Each element will be discussed in turn.

---

[1] *Diagnostic and Statistical Manual of Mental Health Disorders,* Fifth Edition. Washington, DC, American Psychiatric Association, 2013.

The essential feature of PTSD is the development of characteristic symptoms following exposure to one or more traumatic events. The clinical presentation varies. In some individuals, fear-based re-experiencing, emotional, and behavioural symptoms may predominate [2]. The DSM refers to a few mood states of which you may not be familiar with: anhedonia and dysphoria. Anhedonia is defined as *the inability to experience pleasure or have any fun* [3]. Dysphoria is regarded as *a feeling of uneasiness, discomfort, anxiety, or anguish* [4]. It is at this point that it should be noted that in previous editions of the DSM, PTSD was characterised as an anxiety disorder, however it is now placed between *trauma* and *stress-related* disorders.

Before we start analysing the diagnostic features and criteria, I want to reinforce that it is not

---

[2] *Diagnostic and Statistical Manual of Mental Health Disorders,* Fifth Edition. Washington, DC, American Psychiatric Association, 2013.

[3] Durand, V.M. & Barlow, D.H. (2006). Essentials of Abnormal Psychology, Fourth Edition. Thomson Wadsworth, Belmont, CA.

[4] Colman, A.M. (2006). Oxford Dictionary of Psychology, Second Edition. Oxford University Press, New York, NY.

just service personnel who may develop PTSD, indeed it can affect anyone from every walk of life. My personal experience is one of a military background, which has a unique organisational culture and operating environment. Similarly, so do the emergency services, first responders, and the personnel of border protection agencies. Hence, my focus within the handbook will be upon the effects of PTSD within the service culture.

The initial part of the definition of a traumatic stressor is quite clear: *exposure to actual or threatened death, serious injury, or sexual violence.* It is easy for one to identify or acknowledge triggers from the previous statement, particularly for military personnel during their operational service. However, with first responders these waters are somewhat muddied and it may not be easy to identify one specific trigger. Indeed, the PTSD may have developed as a result of an accumulation of numerous traumatic incidents that led to the development of the disorder.

The last part of the initial descriptor is something that requires further discussion: *to an individual, a close family member, or a close friend.* Having previously mentioned that the service culture is unique, I would now suggest that in terms of relationships it is akin to family. The majority of my military tenure was within infantry and special operations units; very close-knit teams particularly at lower levels, where groups comprised a small number of personnel. As with most families, these men and women may not all like each other, but they know the most intimate details about their team members, and the bond between them is extremely strong. These bonds are forged during initial training, mission rehearsal exercises, and reinforced during operational deployments. Notably, it is the latter part of the aforementioned definition that may often be overlooked with regard to the development of PTSD: exposure of a traumatic event to *a close family member, or a close friend.*

Diagnostic Criteria

In the section below, I have summarised the eight diagnostic criteria (A-H) that describe the full symptom picture. Some are quite detailed and others are very simple. Further, some of the elements require two or more of a specific criterion to be present before a diagnosis is confirmed. Leaving this part to the clinicians, I will describe or extrapolate upon the statements within the DSM 5 to give you a greater understanding of the components within the criteria as they have affected me.

A) Exposure to trauma

While deployed to Malaysia, I was involved in a fatal motor vehicle accident. Five of my soldiers were killed and many others seriously injured. My ultimate task was recovery of the bodies back to Australia, which included spending an evening at the morgue and witnessing all five autopsies. Five years later, I was posted back to Malaysia on exchange and the apartment I lived in overlooked the same morgue where I'd spent time with the bodies of my friends. For the next two years, I had no choice but to drive past the accident site every day on the way to and from work.

B) Intrusive symptoms associated with the trauma

My experiences have taken the form of an out of body experience and flashbacks; involuntary memories pop in and out of my consciousness without thought or choice. With the out of body experience I felt like I was floating above myself and looking down upon my body. It was very weird. I have no idea of the trigger for this reaction apart from being overwhelmed by the situation. Flashbacks are common and are usually triggered by one of our senses[5]. In an instant we are taken back to the traumatic event(s): although rationally we know we are in the present, it nonetheless feels like we are back in the moment of a traumatic event and the feelings are extremely real. The most powerful triggers for me are smell and taste, as sight and sound have been desensitised to trauma through movies, TV programs and daily news broadcasts. Further, my understanding is that due to brain anatomy, smell and taste are more closely linked

---

[5] *Diagnostic and Statistical Manual of Mental Health Disorders,* Fifth Edition. Washington, DC, American Psychiatric Association, 2013.

with emotion and memories than vision or hearing, as the olfactory bulb is next to or closely associated with those brain regions. These symptoms can be experienced psychologically or physiologically. My experiences have been feelings of anxiety, depression, helplessness, fear and variations in mood. The physiological symptoms I have felt are increased heart rate, sweating and shaking hands.

C) Avoidance

Certain songs, music or movies summon distressing memories for me. As such, I often change the station or make a conscious decision not to see a specific movie or TV program in order to evade the potential trigger. The smell of fuel plus aromas that are similar to the sickly sweet smell of decaying flesh such as some flowers or perfumes are also odours that I try to avoid. Some of the avoidance techniques I have used at one time or another include staying away from loud noises, congested traffic, public transport and densely populated venues such as shopping centres, sporting events and concerts.

D) Negative thoughts and mood

We all have expectations about others and ourselves; however since I was diagnosed with PTSD I have noticed a heightened view of my expectations and get upset when they aren't met. It can be demoralising when I can't complete activities or tasks that I used to be able to perform with ease. When strangers in particular are not courteous or respectful as I would expect them to be, this will raise feelings of anger within me that are out of proportion to the situation.

Anger is a common emotion following a traumatic event and can become a chronic ailment if not addressed – it certainly did for me. Guilt manifested within me as I questioned why I survived the accident yet several of my colleagues did not. This was often accompanied by shame, where I questioned everything I did during the incident and severely underestimated my effectiveness at the scene and during the recovery of the bodies back to Australia. For example, I constantly asked myself, 'Why didn't I do this? If only I had thought of that.' I also blamed myself for the accident, which was completely irrational. Blaming or second-guessing ourselves doesn't help anyone, least of all ourselves.

I have already mentioned anhedonia, which refers to activities that you used to enjoy that no longer give you pleasure. For me it was no longer playing or watching sport. Sometimes I just couldn't be fucked. It was almost like a sense of martyring myself or even punishing myself, as I didn't deserve to be happy.

Something that did not affect me directly but I did observe in a colleague following our accident in Malaysia, was amnesia. We were in a team of three performing CPR on one of our mates injured in the accident. My colleague has no recollection of me working side by side with him or even being at the scene. To this day he swears I was not there, yet my participation has been validated by many sources.

For members of the services there is a massive rift between 'us' and 'them' (the wider community). No one understands me; they don't 'get' what

I've been through. These feelings extend to our close friendships and family members, often as a defensive measure to prevent ourselves from being hurt by failed relationships. The irony here is that it is this action that directly erodes connectedness and leads to relationship breakdowns. I believe there are two elements to this emotional flaw: firstly, I was unable to experience these emotions; and secondly, I would often punish myself as I considered myself unworthy of happiness, fun or enjoyment.

E) Changes in reactions and response

Most of you will recognise this within yourself or a loved one. I would fly off the handle for no apparent reason with the intensity and frequency of these outbursts being significantly exaggerated. Impulsive and loud noise was the most common element to cause me to lose control with my anger. I also became self-destructive in a number of ways, such as spending money like there was no tomorrow, self-harming, abusing alcohol and sabotaging relationships. Other common behaviours that others might experience include risk-taking, such as speeding in a vehicle or gambling.

I was hyper-vigilant, always scanning for threats even though there weren't any. I could be in a safe environment but I was constantly on the lookout and ready to combat a threat if it presented itself. I would sit with my back to the wall in a café or restaurant in order to see the entry/exit and to ensure no one could approach me from behind. At the movies or theatre I always tried to position myself near the exit so I could make a quick departure, while continually developing plans for all types of 'what if' scenarios. This constant searching, assessing and responding became tiring and psychologically draining. I would overreact to unexpected noises such as a motor vehicle backfiring, an unfamiliar noise at night or someone sneaking up on me. My heart rate would increase and it felt as though my heart was in my throat. In severe cases I would sweat profusely and my hands would tremble.

I also had difficulty concentrating when reading and especially when trying to study. I struggled during conversation, finding it difficult to maintain eye contact as I was forever scanning a room and then losing track of what was being said. This was frustrating for everyone involved. I had difficulty falling asleep or staying asleep if awakened during the night, especially after a nightmare but even if I just had to use the bathroom. This became a vicious cycle where I slept less and less each night but more during the day. I was constantly tired and unable to face the most minute challenges of the day.

F) Symptoms persist longer than one month

This period of one month post the event is what differentiates between Acute Stress Disorder and Post-Traumatic Stress Disorder[6].

---

[6] *Diagnostic and Statistical Manual of Mental Health Disorders,* Fifth Edition. Washington, DC, American Psychiatric Association, 2013.

G) Significant distress and impaired functioning

I was unable to maintain a job and I always felt like the odd one out at social gatherings. When with others in a social setting I really didn't want to be there – everyone else would appear happy but I didn't know how to be like that anymore. Over time, my friends and extended family stopped inviting me to social get-togethers. This didn't affect me at the time but it did impact upon my spouse and children. When I was at my worst, I found it difficult to complete simple tasks such as grocery shopping, paying bills, banking, cooking meals, domestic duties or even maintaining my personal hygiene.

H) Symptoms are not caused by substances

No need for expansion here.

A couple of other points to take into consideration are that the disorder may be long lasting if the stressor or trauma is at the hands of another human, such as in the case of murder or sexual assault. Further, the prospect of developing the disorder may increase when one is located within close proximity to the stressor or if an individual is repeatedly exposed to trauma[7].

This chapter has contained some technical information and clinical definitions that you may not have been familiar with previously. However, I feel it is important to be comfortable with these terms so you can consult effectively with your clinical support team and contribute towards your treatment plan. The following chapters will be much easier to read as they are based on personal experiences with less reliance upon psychological texts.

Comorbid Conditions

Key Points

- The most common comorbid conditions are depression, anxiety, substance abuse, and suicide
- Substance abuse is only a Band-Aid fix

---

[7] *Diagnostic and Statistical Manual of Mental Health Disorders,* Fifth Edition. Washington, DC, American Psychiatric Association, 2013.

- Self-medication is never a wise move
- Suicide is not the answer

Todd: Comorbid conditions are a fancy way to describe the other symptoms you may experience while combatting PTSD. It is important to understand the term, not only for your own benefit but also when conversing with clinicians. This chapter will examine some of the most common comorbid conditions associated with PTSD, namely depression, anxiety, anger, substance abuse, and suicide. There is a fair bit to cover with each of these conditions, so I will break it down respectively.

The most severe of the first three comorbid conditions for me has been depression. A close friend of mine described depression to me as capricious. (Don't worry, I had to Google it too.) The Collins Paperback Dictionary defines capricious as *having a tendency to sudden unpredictable changes in attitude or behaviour*[8]. With regard to psychopathology, I describe capricious as follows: with PTSD I have my known trigger points and I

---

[8] Collins Dictionary (2002). Collins Paperback Dictionary, Fourth Edition. Harper Collins Publishers, Glasgow.

am able to adjust things in my life to compensate for them. However, with depression I can do all the right things and yet it can still pop up out of nowhere and bite me.

Depression

Key points

- Bouts of depression can be devastating
- Eventually it will pass
- Be proactive with your symptom management

Todd: Depression is defined as *a mood disorder in which a person experiences, in the absence of drugs or a medical condition, two or more weeks of significantly depressed moods, feelings of worthlessness and diminished interest or pleasure in most activities*[9]. Over the years I have been able to reverse engineer my PTSD, anxiety, and depressive moments most of the time. Sometimes, however, I am unable to do so with bouts of depression.

---

[9] Myers, D.G. (2006). Psychology, Eighth Edition. Worth Publishers, New York, NY.

This becomes frustrating and feels almost self-defeating. When you are able to reverse engineer or analyse an episode regardless of the condition, you are able to understand it better and it also becomes a form of learning, meaning you are able to move on accordingly. However, when this option is not available to you it can snowball and become much worse than it needs to be.

My advice, at least from a consumer's perspective, is to have faith in your clinicians and your support mechanisms, and just ride it out. It will pass. Easier said than done, I know, but time and experience will support this hypothesis and you will become more comfortable with the onset of symptoms. An open mind and understanding will strengthen your resolve. However, if you are really struggling, seek medical assistance immediately.

Depressive symptoms include *feelings of worthlessness, lethargy, unable to concentrate and a loss of interest in friends, family, and activities*[10].

---

[10] Durand, M.V., & Barlow, D.H. (2006). Essentials of Abnormal Psychology, Fourth Edition. Thomson Wadsworth, Belmont, CA.

Weiten adds further comment to the definition by stating that, *people become socially withdrawn, are less active, tired, experience insomnia, hypersomnia, exhibit a low sex drive and display a decreased appetite*[11].

What does depression look like for me? There is a range of symptoms that affect me. The first that comes to mind is anhedonia. Anhedonia was described in the first chapter and is a clinical term describing the specific behaviour of not enjoying the things in life that you used to enjoy. For me there have been several events that fall into this category such as golf, going to the footy, shopping (not grocery shopping – I have never enjoyed that), exercise, and going to the movies. When I feel the cloud of depression start to overwhelm me, I often just spend the day in bed. My level of apathy can be so high that I just don't have the energy to face the day. The odd blanket day here and there is not a bad thing, however when we start to string a few days or even weeks together, we have a problem.

[11] Weiten, W. (2004). Psychology Themes & Variations, Sixth Edition. Thomson Wadsworth, Belmont, CA.

In my case I generally know what I need to do to get myself out of the mess but, as is often the case, knowledge isn't always the key. I often say to people that the difference between knowledge and action can be like the distance between the Earth and the Moon. I also tend to ruminate; I constantly have negative thoughts circulating in my head, which pop into the forefront of my thoughts. This symptom is unpleasant as it fuels itself both within conscious thought and also within our subconscious.

I also become very insular and hide from the outside world. As such, my communication with loved ones and friends, particularly with my informal support networks, suffers. Sometimes it can be like a form of self-punishment or self-sabotage. I know that reaching out to friends and support networks is not only necessary but also the best form of therapy. Yet, I do nothing about it. I just lock myself away and wallow in self-pity. It's not a nice place to be and I am not a nice person to be around. (Especially for my poor wife – she is such a trooper. I honestly don't know how she puts up with me but I am so glad that she does, as she is my rock. I would be lost without her.) The key here is to be proactive with our symptom management. I now try to exercise everyday, practise mindfulness or meditation, avoid processed food and alcohol, and take my sleep hygiene seriously. What I have found is that this practice keeps the black dog at bay or reduces the effects of depression when it hits me.

Anxiety

Key points

- Anxiety is characterised by excessive worrying about danger or an uncertain future
- Anxiety can be hard to recognise and explain to others

Todd: Anxiety can be as equally debilitating as depression for many. Anxiety is defined as *a marked negative effect and bodily symptoms of tension in which a person apprehensively anticipates* *future danger or misfortune. Anxiety may involve feelings, behaviours, and physiological responses*[12].

Fortunately for me, anxiety no longer has the stranglehold on me that it used to. The strongest element of anxiety for me was separation anxiety. When I was separated from my children, I obviously was not in a position to help them if they needed me. I was a complete mess until I was reunited with them. I was also like this when I was a Company Commander in East Timor – whenever my guys went out on a patrol, my anxiety shot through the roof until they returned to the sanctuary of our Operating Base.

There are a range of symptoms including but not limited to: *excessive worrying, difficulty controlling the worry, restlessness, fatigue, difficulty concentrating, irritability, muscle tension, sleep disturbance, distress or impairment*[13]. I would often worry about the

---

[12] Durand, M.V., & Barlow, D.H. (2006). Essentials of Abnormal Psychology, Fourth Edition. Thomson Wadsworth, Belmont, CA.

[13] Durand, M.V., & Barlow, D.H. (2006). Essentials of Abnormal Psychology, Fourth Edition. Thomson Wadsworth. Belmont, CA.

future and the uncertainty of tomorrow caused me great distress. I couldn't see the light at the end of the tunnel with regard to recovery, which left me wondering, 'What is the point?' I had insomnia and was extremely tired, spending most of the night awake and watching TV alone. I would then spend the majority of the next day asleep and was once more trapped in a vicious cycle. I hated leaving the house and was always on edge in a crowd or an environment that was unknown to me. These issues were difficult to explain to others and it is often equally difficult to identify the symptoms when anxiety first starts to manifest.

Anger

Key points

- Anger is a normal and natural emotion, and the appropriate response in the right situation
- Do not let anger overtake your life
- Find a strategy that helps reduce your anger quickly

- Work on reducing the intensity and frequency of your anger

Todd: This is probably the hardest chapter for me to write – even more difficult than recounting the circumstances that surrounded my attempted suicide. The reason for this is that my outbursts of anger impacted heavily upon those that I loved and cared for the most – my children. They are the innocent victims of PTSD. I have been overly protective of my children, however I could protect them from everyone but me. That was an incredibly difficult realisation and even harder to put down into words.

There were many contributing factors to my anger and extreme outbursts of rage, such as insomnia, irritability, low self-esteem, frustration, and bitterness. These factors were also coupled with the physiological and psychological determinants as outlined later in this chapter. Several environments or situations could trigger an outburst.

Anger, of course, is a normal emotion and in many settings is a legitimate response to a particular situation. However in my case, as with many other people combatting PTSD, these outbursts of anger were not only inappropriate but were extremely intense and way too frequent.

The main triggers for my outbursts were traffic, crowds, and loud or unexpected noise. If I perceived someone to be driving recklessly or dangerously, my anger would go through the roof. It had a physiological effect upon me also; there was a massive knot in my chest and stomach and this sensation would remain with me for hours. Note that my triggers were caused by my perception of what was happening around me, and not necessarily reality. However, when you are deep within the moment it is difficult to distinguish between reality and perception, particularly when you are in a full-on rage.

Crowds would set me off, especially when people were ignorant of others around them and invading my personal space. I did not necessarily go off in these situations but that tightening in my chest and stomach would be present and would remain within me for hours. Loud noises coming out of nowhere were another consistent trigger. Living in a household with three young children was a challenge. Kids make noise whether they are happy, sad, playing or even just watching television. I simply could not handle it. My three boisterous and energetic children were experts at it, although when one of them was removed from the other two, they were as quiet as church mice. I would really lose my shit if one of my children hurt one of the others, regardless of whether or not it was an accident. My anger would fuel itself and escalate, and I would find myself looking for other reasons to be angry.

I remember yelling at my son when he was about ten years of age for some minor infringement and following him around the house, berating him for his actions. He ran into his room and curled up onto his bed. I followed him into his room and kept yelling at him. He looked up at me with tears in his eyes and said, "I came in here to get away from you. I am scared of you!" How do you think this made me feel? Yes, you guessed it, like shit. It was like a simultaneous blow to the head and guts. In that moment I knew that things had to change. I did not want my children living in fear of their dad. They were my little poppets and the centre of my universe. It was devastating to hear those words but when I look back on it now, I am glad that my boy changed me from thinking about anger management to DOING something about it.

Fortunately for my children and me it was not too late. Anger management groups weren't the solution for me; I gave a couple a go but they just made me angry. My psychologist recommended a self-paced workbook on anger management, which was guided by the principles of Acceptance and Commitment Therapy (ACT). It was perfect for me and the timing was just right. I am certainly not saying anger management groups are not effective, indeed quite the contrary. They just didn't work for me at that particular time of my recovery. We are all different and our recovery is a personal journey. Keep an open mind and try all available options until you find what works best for you.

When we are in the middle of an outburst of anger or a full-blown rage, our irrational brain takes over and our cognitive ability diminishes. It can be extremely difficult to reduce one's level of anger when it is that high. The best tip I can give you is to find a technique that reduces your level of anger. For me that is breathing techniques or mindfulness. Long, slow, deep breaths calm my mind and soothe the beast within. Another effective technique is to pay attention to the physiological reactions within your body when you start to get angry and thereafter. As I mentioned earlier it is difficult to calm yourself whilst in a full-blown rage, therefore if you are able to notice the initial change within yourself, the calming techniques are more effective if you implement an effective strategy before it gets to that heightened phase. Give a few techniques a go and practice them when you are calm. It will be easier to implement them when you need it.

Substance Abuse

Key Points

- Substance abuse comes in various forms: alcohol, illicit drugs both soft and hard, and even nicotine
- Addiction can change your personality
- Seek help as soon as you realise you have a dependency

Todd: My drug of choice was alcohol. I started drinking heavily when I was overseas on an exchange posting in Malaysia. I was working as an instructor at the Malaysian Royal Military College, one of the best jobs I ever had in the military. In terms of professional development, job satisfaction, and the lifestyle I had, it was an absolutely brilliant position. The only negative part was that the apartment where I resided over-looked the morgue where I'd spent several days and nights with the bodies of five of my colleagues that were killed in a motor vehicle accident just five years previously. In addition to that I also would drive past the accident site every day to and from work over a two-year period. The drinking became a way to settle my nerves of an evening and to help me get to sleep. I really needed it to help me sleep as the thoughts, images, and trauma of the vehicle accident were always at the forefront of my mind. My ruminations would begin to snowball and then intrusive thoughts would pop into my head at the most inopportune time. Eventually the amount of alcohol I consumed increased, as I needed more and more beer for it to have the desired effect. I also started drinking to numb the pain that I was feeling. This form of self-medication is common; people do it because it works. However, it is only a Band-Aid fix and obviously creates problems of its own.

My alcohol abuse started in 1998-1999 but I was able to manage it and hide it from my work colleagues. It became out of control when I was working in a joint headquarters and living on my own. I didn't have family around me to keep my consumption in check and I started to drink myself to oblivion. Living in Navy accommodation, I had access to alcohol twenty-four hours a day. I drank whatever I could get my hands on – it didn't matter what it was as long as it would soothe the savage beast within. The Navy had an honesty bar, and I am ashamed to say that I wasn't quite so honest with my monetary compensation for the amount of alcohol I consumed each night. This aspect was exceptionally damaging, as I had always prided myself on my honesty and integrity.

When you start to change your character and behaviour, it starts to affect your performance at work and you are unable to hide it from family and friends. This is a strong indicator that the substance abuse has a strong hold on you. If this happens to you don't ignore it: get professional help and fight it. You have always been a fighter and you can overcome this too.

Suicide

Key Points

- Suicide statistic rates for veterans and law enforcement personnel are shockingly high
- The act of suicide will have a profound and devastating effect on all involved
- Suicide is NOT the answer

Todd: Unfortunately suicide is claiming more lives than combat. This is not a phenomenon unique to Australia; the same thing is occurring in the United States, Canada and the United Kingdom. Nor is this occurrence restricted to contemporary veterans; it has been a common manifestation since WWI but it wasn't as openly reported as it is today.

It has been stated that twenty-two serving and ex-serving defence personnel within the United States commit suicide every day. This statistic is absolutely horrific. The reported suicide rates are almost as equally high with law enforcement personnel. My episode with an attempted suicide occurred in November 2009. I had been combatting suicide ideation for a long time and it eventually got the better of me. By this point I had separated from my family and was struggling to live on the periphery of my children's lives. I was overseas and couch-surfing with a close mate of mine who was also going through a separation. I won't divulge the trigger of what changed my suicide ideation to an action plan, as it is not important. However, the subsequent actions and consequences are significant and I feel the need to mention it to warn you of the magnitude.

Once I had decided to end my life and developed a plan with regard to how I would do it, an immense weight was lifted off my shoulders. I felt calm and at peace. It had been a very long time since I had felt either of these emotions. However, let me be clear: SUICIDE IS **NOT** THE ANSWER. I went through the process of writing letters to loved ones stating how much they meant to me and apologising for my pending action. I mentally put everything into order and got down to business.

The next thing I knew, I was in hospital. Two days had passed and I had no idea where I was. When I woke from the coma I had difficulty speaking and could not form sentences properly, my fine motor skills were absent and I had some memory impairment. In addition to the damage that had occurred to me, my suicide attempt also had a profound and damaging effect on my family, particularly my extended family such as my parents and my brother. This, of course, was something that I had not considered – most people don't as the focus is on the self and how to end the pain.

When I reached the point where I could get to grips with what I had done, I become quite philosophical about the whole situation. I had been given a second chance at life: don't let it slip away. However, wanting something and being able to achieve it are two completely different things. Nothing in life worth achieving is easy, however it is worth the effort and can be very rewarding. Hang in there – we are fighters. We have been trained to fight and we need to keep fighting in every aspect of our lives.

The Effect of PTSD on Relationships

Key Points

- You will find out who your true friends are
- Some people will disappoint you and some will surprise you
- Family will make comparisons between the old and the new you
- Cut family members some slack, it is not easy for them either
- Stay connected with the people with whom you served

Todd: *Human beings form groups for a range of reasons such as safety, security, and companionship.*[14] Through our lifespan we create, maintain, and end a large number of relationships. The first we encounter are family, followed by the people in our neighbourhood, school friends, members of sporting teams and ultimately work colleagues.

---

[14] Crisp, R.J. & Turner, R.N. (2010). Essential Social Psychology, Second Edition. Sage Publications, London.

I have heard many people with PTSD say, "You know who your real friends are." Unfortunately this statement is true. But what is sometimes surprising is that there are many people that come into your life and offer you undying support from whom you did not expect. In my newfound outlook on life I try to focus on the positive; as such I do not dwell on the people who have cut me away. I will forever be amazed by the number of kind-hearted people that have entered my life and made a positive impact upon my family and me. It renews one's faith in society and community. This chapter continues with some specific relationships that we have in our lives. Clinical relationships will have their own designated chapter.

Spouse

First and foremost for me is my wife (the current one, by the way). I went through a torrid time in my life after my suicide attempt, including a marriage separation that ultimately lead to divorce, and I was unable to see my children every day. As hard as the separation was at the time, it was not being able to see my kids each day that was the real killer and it was the hardest thing to get used to.

That said, if I hadn't been through that difficult period I would never have met my current wife, Suzy. My goodness, what a wonderful and amazing woman she is! I appreciate that I am biased here, but I want to share some of the things she has done for me and how she has assisted me with my recovery. We met one night at a local pub when we were both drinking. (That in itself was a rarity, as neither of us drinks, so the window of opportunity for us to actually meet was very small indeed.) I was standing on my own, beer in hand and singing along with the music. This little blonde piece walks up to me, pokes my in the chest and says to me, "I can't believe you are singing a George Michael song and you know every freaking word!" I was taken aback and I remember thinking to myself, *Who the fuck are you?* She turned around and off she went. A few minutes later she was back and into me about something else. *Now hang on,* I thought, *she might be interested in me.* And the rest, as they say, is history. It was clearly meant to be.

My first birthday after I had separated from my children was horribly difficult. I woke up in the morning and they weren't with me. It was a hollow and empty feeling. However, that evening I picked my kids up from the house where I used to live with them and we went out for dinner at a local café. Although we were together, it just wasn't the same. There was something missing but I couldn't put my finger on it. After dinner I dropped the kids back to their mother's house and drove over to Suzy's place. Although we weren't living together back then, I just couldn't go home to my spartan one-bedroom apartment. I walked in the front door and sat on the couch. I didn't say anything but Suzy could tell that something wasn't quite right.

"Everything will be OK, Bubba," she said, putting her arms around me and hugging me tightly. Well I lost it; I broke down and cried like a baby. Massive, uncontrollable sobs. I couldn't stop and it got to the point where I could hardly breathe. She must have been thinking to herself, *What have I done?* As strange as it may seem, it was just what I needed. I had been waiting most of my adult life for someone to say that to me. Such a simple gesture had such a profound and cathartic effect on me.

That is just one example of how Suzy has contributed to my recovery. Another thing she did which was of immense benefit was learning about PTSD as soon as she knew of my diagnosis. She Googled it, read the Wikipedia page and bought a few books. In addition we continue to communicate, which is key. Communicating openly and without taking things personally is difficult but definitely worth the effort. She is warm, compassionate, kind, caring, and funny. But enough about her.

On a negative note, I have the propensity to catastrophise. I make mountains out of molehills and when things go bad, I expect the worst. I think it is a natural response given the amount of trauma I have been exposed to, but it is not healthy. It's not good for me and it's not good for my friends and loved ones. When Suzy and I have an argument, which of course is only natural, I used to think our relationship was over. I could feel the pain almost immediately. Fortunately, our relationship wasn't over, but the pain would have an overwhelming grip on me, and my response, like some form of defensive mechanism, was to be a nasty, calculating, hurtful bastard. I would say scathing and spiteful things to Suzy in some childish attempt to hurt her as much as I was hurting. Yet, my hurt was being generated from perception, not from Suzy.

The main point I want to emphasise is that your spouse or partner is on your team. They are in your corner and they are NOT the enemy. It may be difficult at times, but don't take your frustrations out on them and don't underestimate their love and support for you. If they are still in your life, it is a good thing. Frustration can take over for both of you but don't let your inner demons make you doubt your partner's support. Yes, this is easier said than done but it is certainly a goal to work towards.

Family

Relationships with family can be difficult at the best of times but PTSD takes it to a whole new level.

My children, God bless them, have really borne the brunt of my PTSD, anger, frustration, and depression. I am still amazed that they even talk to me, yet with all the hardship they have endured they still love their dad. It just blows me away. I fear that if I were in their shoes, I would never speak to me again. It has also been a testing period for my parents and my brother since becoming aware of my diagnosis. They often remark that they feel helpless and simply don't know what to say to me. It's difficult for family members who knew the old you to be confronted with a new, different you. After my attempted suicide my parents were excellent and so was my brother. Their support was just tiptop during what must have been an extremely disturbing period for them. If I looked at that situation from the perspective of a parent, I would be horrified and dismayed.

What I need to be cognisant of is cutting my family enough slack as I often get frustrated – it is not their fault that my entire world view has changed and theirs hasn't. It's just the way it is.

Friends

Outside of your family unit, your friends are generally the ones who have known you the longest. If, like me, you have drifted away from many or most of your schoolmates, you may find social media to be a great way to re-establish relationships with this element of your relationship community. I have been fortunate enough to reconnect with many friends from my primary and high school years. I initially expected not to have much in common with these people as we all drifted into different parts of society, however I found that it didn't matter. We still had our school years in common and there was much to discuss and laugh about. Good times.

I have also been surprised with the number of friends that have been directly or indirectly touched by mental health disorders. I was amazed. Statistically one in five people will develop a depressive disorder at least once in their lifetime. From a statistical point of view, that means twenty-four of us from my final year in high school will be affected. I have found so many of this group to be supportive, empathetic, and understanding.

Service members

For many people combatting PTSD, your military or first responder colleagues will be one of your best sources of support for you and your family. Unfortunately there will be a small percentage of people with PTSD that are so significantly affected by their service, that people, places, and their former uniform will exacerbate their condition. In this case, I would recommend connecting with a social group outside of your former service organisation.

I consider the informal support networks developed during your time in uniform to be equally as important as the clinical support from your mental health team. When I was medically discharged from the Army I was extremely bitter, not from the discharge itself but the timing of it and how it was handled. In short, it was poor. Here I was, on my own, feeling resentful and angry. I severed all ties with the military. If you were in the Army, used to be in the Army or wanted to be in the Army, then get the freaking hell away from me. I had nothing to do with anyone that had an association with Defence for about eighteen months.

I was later to learn that this enforced separation period was to my detriment. Only my colleagues or mates from the Army understood what I was going through; they 'got' it. Being able to share my experiences with others has been invaluable. I am not necessarily referring to our traumatic experiences but comparing treatment tools that have been effective. Not to mention that it is good to have some mates you can rely on and in turn be in a position to help them.

Why is it that service groups are so strong? *Entitativity is a term that encompasses concepts such as cohesiveness, inter-connectedness, similarity, importance and common goals*[15]. If you have spent any time within a service organisation

---

[15] Crisp, R.J. & Turner, R.N. (2010). Essential Social Psychology, Second Edition. Sage Publications, London.

these characteristics will sound familiar and ring true. The common experiences of service establish strong bonds between its members. Mutual support from your colleagues is a real winner and ultimately satisfying.

Dissolving Past Traumatic Stress
Part I: Finding Support

Seek Inspiration

Key Points

- Motivation and inspiration are key to starting your recovery
- The source of your inspiration is not important
- There are many inspirational people within society

Todd: Inspiration has been an important component of my recovery. Coupled with motivation, it is what gets you started. Inspiration is the driver between wanting something and doing it. Where you source your inspiration or what guides it is not important. Inspiration in itself will be enough to get you off the couch and onto the path of healing.

Initially my children were my source of motivation but at the end of the day, they weren't enough: I needed to get better for *me*. I knew instinctively that if I was doing well then everything else in my life would just fall into place. The source of my inspiration was a recent discovery and it came in two forms: an activity and meeting an inspirational person.

In August 2014 I was fortunate enough to travel to Borneo with eleven other men and women who had been affected by their service. The activity that we undertook as a group was to trek the Sandakan Death March, a 256km route through some of the most inhospitable terrain that Borneo has to offer. When I was informed that I had been selected to participate in the trek, I pulled the book *Sandakan* by Paul Ham off the shelf and started to read it again. I also took notes and drew up a mind map for each chapter. In addition to my interest in the story of Sandakan and the plight of the Prisoners of War (POWs) that were imprisoned there, I wanted to know as much detail as possible about each significant area along the trek.

At the fall of Singapore in February 1942, a number of Australian and British POWs were interred at Changi. However, there were already thousands and thousands of POWs being imprisoned within Changi Gaol. A force of several thousand were sent to Burma and Thailand to work on the infamous Burma/Thai railway. An additional group known as B Force was sent to Borneo to be imprisoned at Sandakan. These POWs were tortured and beaten during their captivity and some were even murdered. Those that survived their captivity were systematically starved for two and a half years. As the Second World War came to a conclusion in the Pacific, the Japanese wanted no evidence of their maltreatment of the POWs, so their solution was to march the POWs to their deaths. At this stage the majority of prisoners weighed approximately 40kg and were used as forced labour to transport food, water, and stores to Ranau, some 256km away. The route between the two towns had been constructed by the local tribesmen who thought the track was for the Japanese, so it was an indirect route and covered difficult terrain. The POWs travelled the distance without footwear, shirts or hats, and endured the worst environment that Borneo had to offer. There were three death marches in total and of the 1,400 men that undertook the marches, only six survived. These men were able to evade their captors by hiding in the jungle and finding support from the local population. The mortality rate was 99.5%; those men that rested for too long or who could not get to their feet were beaten or bayoneted to death and the fortunate ones met their demise with a bullet. Two hundred bodies were never recovered.

Walking in the footsteps of these brave men was a solemn and life-changing experience. For me it was like walking through a graveyard, and as I was trekking with former soldiers I often thought of the mates that I had lost. It truly put things into perspective and proved to be an excellent and inspiring activity. I was reconnected with soldiers again and walking in the footsteps of our forebears who were systematically starved for two years and eventually murdered. Yes, I had a lot of challenges in my life and faced a lot of difficulties on a daily basis, but things could be much, much worse.

The second source of my inspiration was meeting a bloke by the name of Paul de Gelder, while speaking at a corporate event. Paul was a former soldier like myself but he transferred to the Navy and became a clearance diver. Most Australians will be familiar with Paul, if not with his name then certainly what happened to him one day in Sydney Harbour. He was swimming in the harbour while the Defence Science and Technology Organisation (DSTO) were conducting tests on surface swimming radar. A large and aggressive bull shark attacked Paul, culminating in the loss of his hand, most of his upper right thigh, and a serious amount of blood. His right forearm and eventually his right leg were amputated.

Paul came face to face with death and managed to pull through. Surviving the shark encounter and subsequent surgery was only half the battle, as he then needed to learn to live, walk, and function normally again. His recovery is an amazing story of resilience, determination, and hard work. He is an exceptionally impressive man and meeting him was the catalyst for me to get my life in order.

Inspirational people come from all walks of life, and it does not matter where you source your inspiration or motivation to combat PTSD. All that matters is that you make a conscious decision to get on with your life. I appreciate it that it is not that simple, however taking that first step is profound. Keep moving forward.

Peer Support

Key Points

- Peer support is powerful
- Mutual support is the aim
- Formal support groups are a great resource

Todd: The powerful medium of peer support is essential with regard to living a positive and fulfilling life. Within this section I am going to focus on the Army and part of its organisational culture, only because it is what I'm familiar with.

When you march into the Army, teamwork and mateship are inculcated into you right from the get-go. Teamwork, teamwork, teamwork – you NEVER let your mates down. Using the Australian infantry model, each platoon comprises three sections of nine men and a small headquarter element of three personnel. The sections are then broken down into three groups of three. The groups and sections all provide mutual support to one another. The lowest level is the buddy system. Just you and one other bloke; you are responsible for him and he is responsible for you. You NEVER let your mate down, and it doesn't matter whether you like each other or not, you are both professionals and you have a job to do. Regardless of what service you are from and how long you have spent in uniform, you already know how to look after one another. Now that you are out of uniform there is absolutely no reason why you can't continue this level of support to each other.

There is literally a plethora of formal support groups within the community. They don't necessarily have to be ex-service organisations, although that would be my recommendation for the majority of us. For those of you for whom the military itself exacerbates the condition, I would recommend a community-based PTSD support group. I consider informal support networks to be just as important as the formal support groups.

My informal network comprises a few fellow PTSD sufferers but they are located all over the country so we keep in regular contact via telephone and SMS. I am fortunate to have a couple of close mates in my hometown. These are my go-to guys as nothing beats a face-to-face catch up. There are significant benefits to this, such as sharing a laugh, getting out of the house, plus from a support perspective you can read one another's facial expressions and body language. Anyone can bullshit you via a text message but it is far more difficult to do it with someone sitting directly in front of you.

The final avenue I want to discuss is social media, particularly Facebook. For the veteran community it is a great way to keep in touch with brothers that are spread all over the country or overseas, and can also be a great way to support each other too. Group discussions about coping strategies, effective treatment and so on can be enlightening and beneficial. However, a word of warning: Facebook can be a double-edged sword. My suggestion is that you are cautious and particular with whom you share your stories. Many people out there focus only on the negative and constantly post the same complaints and whinge about the same problems over and over and over. This stuff used to really grind me down. In order to change our situation we need to do something about it. Whinging on Facebook will not help our recovery; in fact it will exacerbate it. Look after your mates and check in with them regularly. Don't be afraid to ask them tough questions and if you feel that you can't help, find someone who can. It might be another mate, a clinician or an Emergency Department. If need be have the courage to call the police if you are worried about one of your friends.

Clinical Support

Key points

- If you haven't done so already, seek professional help, starting with your GP or local doctor.
- If you have a clinical support team comprising more than one professional, make sure they are talking to each other and are on the same page.
- You don't have to like your clinician but you must have faith and trust in them. If you don't then get a new one.
- If your doctor recommends medication, do not view this as a failure. By all means do your research on the suggested medication but do not view it as a cure all. The correct medication may take a while to take effect – be patient and communicate with your doctor.

Todd: Clinical support is essential in the treatment of PTSD and its comorbid conditions. If you are seeing a few different clinicians, try to get them to communicate with each other, even if you have to co-ordinate a teleconference with them. I feel it is essential for your clinical support team to be on the same page; there is nothing worse than having them heading in different directions. It is also important for you to be involved with the development of your treatment plan. It is empowering and you are making a positive contribution to your own recovery.

Types of Therapy

- CBT – Challenging thoughts and beliefs
- TE – Verbalising feelings in the moment
- ACT – Directly addressing behaviour
- EMDR – Developing new neural pathways around trauma

The following descriptions are necessarily basic, and your clinician will be able to provide you with a fuller account of each type of therapy. Please note you don't have to like your Psychiatrist, Psychologist or General Practitioner, however you MUST have faith in them and trust them. If you don't, then it's time to find someone else.

Cognitive Behavioural Therapy (CBT)

CBT is widely used with regard to the treatment of mental disorders. CBT is defined as *a popular integrated therapy that combines cognitive therapy (changing self-defeating thinking) with behaviour therapy (changing behaviour)*[16]. In a nutshell it is about challenging our thoughts and modifying our behaviours accordingly. We often have the propensity to go off half-cocked or misread a situation. CBT encourages us to break down a situation that has been presented to us and to analyse the possible outcomes or reasons for a particular scenario playing out before us. For example, we see a mate down the street and they do not return your wave. Instead of perceiving that we have been snubbed and that this person is an

---

[16] Myers, D.G. (2006). Psychology, Eighth Edition. Worth Publishers. New York, NY.

arsehole, we need to have a look at the possible reasons why our friend did not acknowledge us. Such as, they may not be wearing their glasses/contact lenses and didn't see us. They may have a lot on their mind with work. One of their kids might be sick and they are in a hurry to collect him from school. We could go on and on with examples but that's not the point here. Once we have analysed these possible reasons we can modify our behaviour accordingly. So, instead of assuming the old mate who ignored us is an arsehole, we cut him a bit of slack and are no longer in a foul mood for the rest of the day.

Therapeutic Enactment (TE)

I undertook TE treatment a few years ago with a group of clinicians from Canada. Dr Marvin 'Marv' Westward had developed this form of therapy over a fifteen-year period and found it was very effective with veterans. The ten-day program began with introductions and bonding between the participants, and gaining trust with each other and with the clinicians and the process. Each of us in turn identified a traumatic event from our service, which was re-enacted to help us gain some closure. Let me be clear that it was **NOT** role-plays. The staff dissected each situation before guiding each participant through their respective enactment. Key people surrounding the traumatic event were performed by the other participants and clinical support team. We were steered through the scene and told what to say or verbalise our feelings.

Another element outside the counselling and therapy paradigm was touch. When it was required, we were supported physically during the enactment. In addition to the enactment we worked on goal-setting and integrating back into society, not just with jobs but with rewarding careers. Personally I thought the program was excellent and I got so much out of the experience. It is a shame that the Australian veteran community does not have a Dr Marv Westward and his program readily available.

Acceptance and Commitment Therapy (ACT)

I undertook a self-paced ACT treatment in an attempt to curb my anger. I had tried anger management programs in group settings but guess what, it just made me angry. Go figure. A psychologist recommended the ACT treatment to me and it was very effective. Of course it wasn't an overnight success and it took a fair bit of hard work but it was definitely worth the effort and I am a much better person for it. I still lose my shit every now and then – at the end of the day I am only human – but the frequency between episodes is significantly greater and the intensity at which I fly off the handle has reduced a great deal. The result for me is quite clearly successful.

Eye Movement Desensitisation and Reprocessing (EMDR)

Leading psychiatrist and founder of the Trauma Centre in Boston, Bessel van der Kolk M.D., has spoken of EMDR having great success among people living with PTSD. At the time of writing, I am about to embark upon my first EMDR treatment plan, and I am excited about it. The aim here is developing new neural pathways around trauma. I will be dealing with some events that haven't been fully processed and are still causing me anxiety and stress. Fortunately most of the traumatic events I have experienced have been processed through the above treatments.

For EMDR to be effective you must have complete faith in your therapist. The first stage is to set up a 'safe place' in your mind. This is based on an event or picture from your past that has brought you peace or happiness. The reason for this is twofold: it keeps you grounded before the session starts, then if you become distressed during the treatment you go to your safe place to reduce your distress. Reducing your distress is what assists you to develop the new neural pathways around your traumatic event.

Psychopharmacology

Well, folks, this will be quite short. I am not a doctor or psychiatrist and as such I do not dare to delve into this area except to relate my personal experience. I am on a variety of medications for numerous disorders. People often ask me, "Are they effective?" At the risk of sitting on the fence, they are what you need them to be. I would like to quote a good friend of mine called Shane, who summed it up perfectly when he said, "Antidepressants may not solve the issue, however they turn the sharp pain within me to a dull ache." Medication is not a silver bullet producing a magical and effortless solution, but when it is combined with counselling, mindfulness, and regular exercise, we are on to a winner. Sometimes the right medication takes trial and error and unfortunately it may take a while to get it right. In addition, you may start to display the side effects of the medication before it starts to take effect. Consult with your doctor and have faith in their experience and knowledge.

How Pets Can Help

Key points

- Pets can be great companions and service dogs can assist you in public
- They are intuitive and can read your mood
- They have a wonderful stabilising effect on your disposition
- They can be the difference between suicide ideation and a suicide plan

Todd: Many of us have grown up with pets in the household and for the majority, our pets are also considered to be a member of the family. During my childhood we had a dog, a cat, and a guinea pig as pets. My preferred pet was the dog – there is something about dogs that gives me a sense of calm and reassurance. They are renowned as great companions but my dogs have also been much more than that to me, especially my current dog.

Digby is not your run of the mill 'man's' dog, indeed he is far from it, being what many would refer to as a 'hairdresser's' dog. He is a small labradoodle but he makes up for his diminutive stature with his personality. He is cheeky, smart – possibly too smart for his own good – and incredibly playful. He is not technically an assistance dog but he is able to read my mood well. By way of example, if I am sad or depressed he becomes tactile, either sitting on my lap or laying his head on my leg. When I start to get angry, I sometimes notice it in Digby's body language before I notice it within myself: he moves away from me and does not look comfortable at all. He has even woken me at night when I have had a hypo (a drop in blood glucose levels dangerous for diabetics) in my sleep. If it happened once or twice I would have attributed it to coincidence, but it has now happened around six times. He sleeps in our room and wakes me by scratching the door. I always assume that he needs to go outside to do his business but as I sit upright and walk to the door, I notice the tell-tale signs. Pretty amazing.

It really doesn't matter what your preference for a pet is, but when you are on your own day after day recovering from physical or psychological wounds, a pet can be the perfect source of companionship. My son, for example, keeps frogs and a lizard. Now they aren't my cup of tea but he loves them to bits and that's all that matters. My wife openly states that Digby has saved my life on a few occasions.

Looking into Digby's eyes or observing his playful nature has an overwhelming effect upon me. Is it a distraction or a form of mindfulness? I am not sure to be honest, but while I am focusing on my dog I find myself in the now, there is nothing else going on, and there is no negative chatter in the back of my head. It's just me and my dog – one of my best mates. Whether we are on the couch watching television together or whether he is at my feet while I am working on the computer, he is always with me. He is extremely embarrassing on the lead though, which is why we always run together at night. He is well behaved inside the house and in the backyard, but as soon as we cross the threshold of the front door he is like a demon possessed! He is my boy and I am extremely proud of him.

Plenty of organisations offer service dogs to former members of the Defence Force and Emergency services, as they provide so many benefits for their owners. Often it is the service dog that enables people to increase their confidence or to summon the courage to leave the house. While in unfamiliar territory or in a crowded area like a shopping centre, the service dog will help the owner to feel at ease, reducing their psychopathology to a level where they can carry out tasks effectively. The options here in Australia are to apply for a fully trained dog or if you already have a dog, it can be trained to meet the specific requirements for the respective course. In addition to training your dog, you will also be taught how to handle it successfully.

Resilience and Hope

Key points

- Resilience is an effective tool at our disposal
- Keep healthy
- Don't lose hope

- Fight with everything you have
- Never give up

Todd: Resilience is an awesome tool to have at our disposal when we are combatting PTSD or any other form of psychopathology. The difficulty with it, of course, is that it is hard to achieve and easy to lose.

In my teenage years and prior to joining the Army, I was a resilient young man, every obstacle was just water off a duck's back. Compared to the traumatic events that I was exposed to while serving, I really didn't encounter many difficulties in life. However, when you are young and with little life experience behind you, everything seems like a big deal. In my youth I was fortunate enough to be able to bounce back and get back on my feet with ease. The same could be said when I enlisted into the Army and undertook respective recruitment and initial employment training. I was able to approach every experience, be it positive or negative, with the same amount of enthusiasm and gusto. Bring it on! Officer training was a whole new level yet I didn't struggle or doubt my ability – I was confident that I would complete my training to a high standard and be rewarded with my Corps of choice upon graduation. Admittedly, I did possess a considerable chip on my shoulder about my background and my new environment. Nonetheless, I just got on with it.

The first real challenge I faced in life was the death of four friends, fellow officer cadets at the Royal Military College. These guys died in a light aircraft accident. Yours truly was supposed to be with them yet as fate would have it, I was needed elsewhere and one of the other boys took my place. At the time I tried to shrug it off and pretend that it didn't affect me. Looking back I now know it did affect me – of course it did – I had just lost four mates in the blink of an eye. Here were four young, intelligent and strong men that passed away so quickly. It didn't exactly turn my world upside down but I did start to challenge my view on life. I remember regularly wondering, *What is the point?* I questioned everything: life, the Army, my role in the universe, what I was doing ... Some serious questions were being asked and I didn't have the answers, at least not then.

The big question that didn't occur to me at the time was, *How do we build our resilience?* Following on from building or establishing resilience is how to maintain it. We will get to that in a moment. Two years after the aircraft accident came the vehicle accident in Malaysia where five of my colleagues were killed. Now that did turn my world upside down. The negative and intrusive thoughts from the plane crash just two years before seemed to be reinforced by the accident and my involvement in it. My entire world view changed; everything that I had considered to be true was now false. Life was fragile and bordering upon futile. These were difficult times indeed.

So what turned my thoughts around and how did I develop resilience? Good question. It certainly didn't happen overnight and there was a lot of trial and error over the next twenty years. In my opinion it hasn't been just one thing – it has been a combination of therapy, medication, and a new mindset developed from yoga and mindfulness.

Regular exercise has been critical in maintaining a stable mood and mitigating the negative affects of PTSD, anxiety, and depression. As 'they' say: healthy body, healthy mind.

The next element to approach is hope. Unfortunately there was a time in my life when all hope was gone; I had expended all of my hope currency and I was left bankrupt. I just could not see a light at the end of the tunnel with regard to recovery. I had made much progress over the years but there was always something dragging me back into the pit of misery that my life had become. I was exhausted and just gave up, but fortunately I was given a second chance. Hope is such a powerful yet underestimated quality in recovery. My advice is to cling to it with everything you have, no matter how small it appears. Try to think of hope as a helium balloon on a string: it doesn't take much physical effort to hold onto it, but once you let go, it is gone forever. This may not be the case for everyone, but it certainly was for me. Please take my word for it and don't go testing my hypothesis. I do consider this analogy to be the case for the majority of us. Please, hang in there with everything you have and fight tooth and nail to cling to hope. We are fighters, we have been trained to fight, and we need to approach recovery or life with the same combative qualities.

Placing Value on Trust

Key points

- Your loved ones usually act in your best interest, even if it doesn't feel like it at the time
- Be open to the suggestions of others
- Vicarious trauma may also affect those closest to you

Rob: Your family, friends, and supporters want to see you be well mentally and physically. Not only for your own sake, but for theirs too. They feel your pain. Until you sit back and still the mind for a while, reflecting on your life and the ripple effect it causes, it's hard to realise that people just want you to have the best care available and to be consistently happy and at peace.

Trust your supporters and try some of the ideas suggested to you. Use your discretion and be open to their suggestions. After all, good intentions are unlikely to be harmful.

It is often human nature and part of self-preservation to ignore or question others' personal suggestions towards you. We all tend to have an 'I know best' attitude. When loved ones and people that care for you can see how uncomfortable your situation has become, it is difficult for them to hold back and not say anything. Because family, friends, and supporters are empathetic, they feel your suffering too. Vicarious trauma (second-hand trauma) may also affect people closest to you.

The ripple effect takes place when those who care about you tell their workmates, shopkeepers, hairdressers, and community groups that they are frustrated, sad, and hurt about not being able to make a greater impact on your wellness. In turn, these people mention to others that they know of someone suffering from post-traumatic stress, and how sad it is they can't be helped, and so on.

Now, you may be on your road to recovery by figuring out 'how' by yourself, or you may have been brave and open enough to follow the guidance offered from loved ones. In that case, this chapter may be just a friendly reminder or non-applicable to you. It is also worth carefully considering the advice given by your medical practitioner about an integrative approach to wellness and recovery. More and more recent research and evidence-based study is suggesting that natural therapies are proving to be more effective than synthetic chemicals to calm the mind and heal the body.

So take a chance on incorporating a piece of advice given to you recently that you may not have acted on yet but have heard suggested before. You never know until you give it a go! Keep persisting until you get some new results. Trying something only one or twice may not be enough to help dissolve post-traumatic stress.

Action Plan

- Ask the person closest to you to repeat the last thing they suggested to help you recover from post-traumatic stress
- Act on the caring advice/suggestion previously given to you by your loved one
- Next time you see a loved one, give them a hug and say THANK YOU

Volunteering: The Importance of Giving Back

Key points

- Research shows that formal volunteering reduces the effects of psychopathology, including depression and anxiety
- Volunteering is good for the soul and increases wellbeing
- Join a support network and, when you are able, start supporting others
- There must be a good fit between you and the volunteer organisation

Todd: After leaving the Army I was lost. I was no longer a member of an organisation and as such I did not have regular contact with other people. Although I was undertaking part-time study with the ultimate goal to become a clinical psychologist, I was not among like-minded people and became withdrawn and insular.

A little over twelve months before writing this book, I had a conversation with the former Chief of Army in Australia, General Peter Leahy. General Leahy was the Chairman of the charity Soldier On and he suggested that I should get in touch with the CEO, Mr John Bale, about doing some volunteer work with the organisation. I deliberated and mulled it over for a few months and then finally took the plunge. It was one of the best decisions I have ever made. Since working with Soldier On as a volunteer, I have experienced numerous benefits with regard to recovery and general wellbeing.

I mentioned earlier that for the seven years post my medical discharge from the Australian Defence Force, I felt lost and alone. Being a member of the Soldier On team gave me a sense of belonging.

Every time I went into the Reintegration Centre in Canberra, the whole team made me feel welcome and were glad to see me. Now even if this was an act it was nonetheless very nice and slowly started to rebuild my self-esteem. The volunteer work also gave me a sense of purpose; I was involved with an organisation that was helping Australia's service men and women. I was no longer on my own. Although I was only a small cog in a much larger machine, I was helping our wounded warriors in an indirect way. My administrative support to the Chief Operations Officer, Karlie Brand, also made me feel like I was contributing to society again. For the most part, since leaving the Army I had always felt like a burden on society but now I was doing my part for the cause. It was a significant turn around from how I viewed my outlook on life and myself. If you get the opportunity to do something similar I would encourage you to do it.

The only warning I would give you before you embark on formal volunteer work is that you must find an organisation and a task that fits with you. My first stint within the volunteer world was as a guide at the Australian War Memorial (AWM) in Canberra. The AWM is the brainchild of the War Correspondent from WWI, Charles Bean. It is both a memorial to Australia's fallen and a museum. It was a fantastic organisation to be a part of, and I took the necessary steps to become a volunteer guide. I was accepted and undertook a demanding three-month course on the AWM's history, learning how to take a ninety-minute guided tour. I absolutely loved every aspect of it ... except guided tours have people in them. I couldn't face my audience. Go figure.

This came at a time when my PTSD was particularly debilitating. I had lost my self-esteem and resilience. I had no tolerance for problems or problematic people; in short I did not play well with others. So my newfound career as a volunteer ended as quickly as it began. Unfortunately this experience deterred me from trying something else for a long time. What I found worked best for me at Soldier On was doing things behind the scenes where I only had to interact with people I knew and with whom I was comfortable. Of course, the examples highlighted above are purely anecdotal at best, and I would now like to examine some relevant academic studies.

The data for the majority of studies outlined below comes from the Americans' Changing Lives (ACL) study. The ACL is a nationally representative sample of adults twenty-five years of age or older, who lived in the United States. In their paper on volunteering and depression, Musicka and Wilson[17] suggest that there are a number of explanations why volunteering may produce benefits for individuals suffering from depression or anxiety. Although the paper focuses upon the elderly, it is assumed that these findings can be translated to the younger members of society who have the time available to dedicate to formal volunteering, particularly the contemporary veteran. Musicka

---

[17] Musicka, M.A., & Wilson, J.B. (2002). Volunteering and depression: the role of psychological and social resources in different age groups. Collaborative effort between The University of Texas and Duke University. [Electronic version. Date accessed 28 January 2015].

and Wilson[18] identify that volunteer work improves access to social and psychological resources, which are proven methods of countering the effects of negative moods and psychopathology. Further, some of the effects of volunteering on depression are attributable to the social integration it encourages. In a study conducted by Yunqing and Ferraro (2005)[19], the authors found that their results revealed a beneficial effect of formal volunteering on depression, but not for informal helping. However, a point to note that is significant to the physically wounded within the veteran community is that functional health problems emerged as a central obstruction to volunteering.

[18] Musicka, M.A., & Wilson, J.B. (2002). Volunteering and depression: the role of psychological and social resources in different age groups. Collaborative effort between The University of Texas and Duke University. [Electronic version. Date accessed: 28 January 2015].

[19] Yunqing, L., & Ferraro, K.F. (2005). Volunteering and Depression in Later Life: Social Benefit or Selection Processes? *Journal of Health and Social Behaviour.* [Electronic version. Date accessed: 30 January 2015].

The positive relationship between volunteering and wellbeing has been widely understood as evidence of the productive effect of volunteering. Using data from the ACL survey, the study conducted by Yunqing and Ferraro (2006)[20] examined the relationships among volunteering, functional limitations, and depressive symptoms during middle and later adulthood. Their findings reveal a valuable effect of volunteering in later life. In addition, Wheeler, Gorey, and Greenblatt[21] conducted a meta-analysis of thirty-seven independent studies; their findings indicated that volunteers' sense of wellbeing seemed to be significantly bolstered through volunteering.

---

[20] Yunqing, L., & Ferraro, K.F. (2006). Volunteering in Middle and Later Life: Is Health a Benefit, Barrier or Both? *New Jersey Department of Health and Senior Services*. Purdue University. [Electronic version. Date accessed: 30 January 2015].

[21] Wheeler, J.A., Gorey, K.M, & Greenblatt, B. (1998). The Beneficial Effects of Volunteering for Older Volunteers and the People they Serve: A Meta-Analysis. *The International Journal of Aging and Human Development. Volume 47,* Number 1.

Further, Borgonovi[22] proposed that volunteering might contribute to happiness levels through increased empathy. These findings are particularly salient when volunteers are assisting individuals who are considered 'worse off' than the volunteer. Joongbaeck and Manacy[23] also found that volunteering affects the decline of depression for individuals above age sixty-five.

The aforementioned studies highlight a causal link between volunteering and reducing the rates of depression and anxiety within the community. However, the volunteer work must be of a formal nature. Although these studies focus upon individuals over the age of sixty-five, it is assumed that these benefits are realised because it is this segment of society that is able to commit to regular volunteer work. One can therefore extrapolate that these benefits for reducing depression and

[22] Borgonovi, F. (2008). Doing well by doing good. The relationship between formal volunteering and self-reported health and happiness. *Social Science & Medicine. Volume 66,* Issue 11.

[23] Joongbaeck, K., & Manacy, P. (2010). Volunteering and Trajectories of Depression. *Journal of Ageing and Health.* [Electronic version. Dated accessed: 28 January 2015].

anxiety combined with raising general wellbeing can also be translated to the contemporary veteran community, who are unable to undertake full time work due to their service.

Action Plan:

- If you have time, make a commitment to volunteer for an organisation
- Approach the chosen organisation expressing your interest
- Volunteer for one hour per week to start with and devote your time as a volunteer to your chosen organisation
- Encourage others you know living with PTSD to also volunteer for an organisation

Homeostasis

Key points

- Maintaining a state of equilibrium takes conscious and physical effort
- When our mood is high it will dip

- Be prepared for this by implementing mitigating strategies

Homeostasis is defined as *a state of physiological equilibrium or stability*[24]. It can be likened to a thermostat in our homes, which is set at a comfortable temperature. When the temperature within the house reaches this preferred zone, the heating element ceases to produce the hot air that warms our house. Eventually the temperature within the dwelling will drop because the heating element is not producing hot air. Once the air temperature reduces to a certain level, the thermostat kicks in again, producing more hot air. This cycle continues while the heating element and internal thermostat is switched on. Our bodies work in a similar way with heat; you will notice that during physical exertion our bodies produce heat and we perspire. Our sweat is designed to cool our bodies down[25], just like the aforementioned thermostat. Another example

[24] Weiten, W. (2012). Psychology Themes & Variations, Sixth Edition. Thomson Wadsworth, Belmont, CA.

[25] Weiten, W. (2012). Psychology Themes & Variations, Sixth Edition. Thomson Wadsworth, Belmont, CA.

is with thirst. When our bodies start to become dehydrated, our bodies let us know that we are feeling thirsty. Our preferred level of hydration has dipped, we become thirsty and then we drink fluid to maintain equilibrium within our body. Hunger works in the same manner. Of course, these are basic examples and descriptions but hopefully you can see my point.

Homeostasis also occurs with our mental state and our mood, and it is important to be aware of this when in the recovery period of PTSD and thereafter. Indeed, it happened to me recently. I had an awesome day. I participated in an event called the RAW Challenge; based on a military obstacle course covering seven kilometres with forty-plus obstacles. I completed the course with a team of friends from High School, and had the best morning. It was great fun. Later that evening I attended a school reunion. I'm not really into reunions; in fact this was the first school reunion I had been to. It had been thirty years since I had seen some of these people. However, I had a brilliant night. Even though it was at a pub, there was loud music, and a lot of people drinking excessively, I strangely did not feel uncomfortable. The entire day was fantastic. I was riding a wave of an almost euphoric state for over twelve hours.

But the next day arrived and I felt the exact opposite. Bang! I was now in a dip, which was needed to bring my mental state and mood back into equilibrium. However, unlike the examples I mentioned earlier, the mental version of homeostasis can take a lot longer to level out. This recent example took me about ten days.

I feel that it's important to be aware of homeostasis so you can prepare for the inevitable dips, make a plan, and implement some mitigating strategies to ensure that you don't drop into a state of full-blown depression. The first time I experienced this dip after a great event was after catching up with some mates from the Army, an informal reunion. It was so good seeing these blokes again, but unfortunately I really struggled for a few weeks after the event. I didn't know what was going on until a psychologist explained this phenomenon to me. Keep this in your kit bag and be prepared for it.

Action Plan

- Increase your sessions with your psychologist when you sense your equilibrium is about to be challenged
- Mindfulness or meditation can help you deal with the dips
- Maintain an exercise routine so that your body is balanced and fit
- Maintain a clean and healthy diet so you are not adversely affected by unnatural foods and additives

Dissolving Past Traumatic Stress
Part II: Making Sense of Mindfulness

What Happens in the Brain

Key Points

- Trauma affects the brain at a deep level
- Flashbacks, insomnia, and nightmares can be triggered by sensory experiences
- It is possible to rebuild the damaged neural network and to retrain the brain to experience memories in a different way using mindfulness

Rob: The brain has approximately 100 billion nerve cells, which form over a trillion connections called synapses. So it is no wonder that when some people experience or witness a traumatic event, that major organ can be deeply affected and not so easily healed. Because the mind stores the sequence of the event and the relationship to the brain invokes feedback loops, it is no surprise that flashbacks, insomnia, nightmares, and bad memories keep recurring.

The five senses of sight, sound, taste, touch, and particularly smell interact between the mind and the brain. So it makes sense when you hear about someone affected by PTSD say that months and even years after a devastating experience, the scent of perfume, the sound of a loud, banging noise, the taste of a certain food, or the texture of a material triggers a flashback. When this happens, the Fight-or-Flight response kicks in, the stress hormone, cortisol, is secreted in the brain and the physical body experiences discomfort, causing feelings of anxiety and depression. This may be stating the obvious for some people, however it is important to recognise the simple sequence of events that continues to cause suffering among human beings who have been injured physically or psychologically.

The good news is that the brain can heal itself and does not have to be overruled by the primitive reactions of fear, anger, and aggression. The brain is constantly evolving and when injured, neurons and synapses try to reconnect and in turn rebuild the damaged neural network.

These nerve cells – also known as neurons – are responsible for remodelling connections in the brain after an injury in a form scientifically known as neuroplasticity. And when PTSD sufferers expose themselves to new experiences like yoga, a mindfulness practice, jogging, painting or writing, just to name a few examples, neuroplasticity is given an increased probability of occurring. Even better, when someone is passionate and enthusiastic about learning again, new neural pathways will form and the brain can continue to repair and evolve. So to continue producing new nerve cells, physical activity, mentally stimulating exercises, and social interaction is highly recommended.

A few former military wounded warriors I have worked with as a Mindfulness Coach over the years advised me that they were trained to avoid dangerous situations that threaten the lives of themselves and others whilst neutralising conflict to protect people who need help. As we discussed the Fight-or-Flight response, some wounded warriors told me they were wired more on the Fight side of this fence.

The reptilian part of the brain is largely responsible for actions associated with fighting and fleeing. These instinctive reactions are built into the lower brain's structure that includes the amygdala and the hippocampus. In some people, when the memory of the traumatic experience surfaces in the mind, the Fight-or-Flight response is triggered and a secretion of cortisol is released in the amygdala and hippocampus region. At this point the physical body is affected with a degree of paralysis, intrusive thoughts, irritability, and rage. The reptilian brain has no control built into it and this is why you hear about people who have acted in a fit of uncontrollable rage or sorrow only to regret their actions later on.

The brain's limbic system is the 'emotions headquarters' and also related to the sense of smell and long-term memory. Memory is so powerful it makes emotions extremely sticky in the brain. I heard a wounded warrior who has served his country at war say that the smell of sweet perfume reminds him of the smell of decaying flesh related to a traumatic event experienced several years ago. Memories are inherently difficult to remove and many times, with the best of intentions, trauma still lingers and remains vivid. Over time this is compounded with the frustration that post-traumatic stress keeps reappearing despite continued effort and an integrative approach to the sufferer's healthcare, resulting in a potential downwards spiral.

The good news is that with a regular mindfulness practice, these memories begin to fade and become less intense over time. So if the affected person can start with their consciousness observing the feelings of anger, frustration or anxiety, an emotional gap between consciousness and the mind is created. From there, be patient and allow the feeling to come and go, whilst taking a few deeper breaths in and out. This breathing technique allows the parasympathetic nervous system to bring the brain into a calmer state of being and into the present moment.

To rise above the lower brain and access the higher brain for a solution to post-traumatic stress, it is encouraged to ask the following questions:

1. Are these challenges that need fixing, tolerating or escaping from?
2. Who can I talk to that has solved a similar life challenge effectively?
3. How can I access my true self / consciousness for the answers?

In order to access the higher brain, it is important to be physically rested and to stay away from triggers that can cause unpleasant memories to emerge. Then, by finding a suitable space for a few minutes every day in a relaxing environment, come to stillness either seated, kneeling or lying down, and simply become mindful, observing one breath at a time whilst looking and listening to your surroundings. There is no need for your eyes to be closed. Eventually, your inner space will be accessed and this can be felt by a deeper sense of calm and tranquillity. Thoughts may come and go during this mindfulness practice and, with the best intentions, witnessed in a non-judgemental way before focusing on the next breath. Only the higher brain and being conscious in the present moment can detach the mind from emotional reactions. When mindfulness is practiced on a regular basis, the brain eventually undergoes a positive transformation towards a new way of being.

What Happens in the Body

Key Points

- Positive images, feelings or thoughts release endorphins in the brain that can heal the body at a cellular level

- Negative images, feelings or thoughts release cortisol, which can damage the body in both the medium and long term
- Focusing on the breath and practising being in the present moment using mindfulness can increase the amount of endorphins and decrease the amount of cortisol released

Rob: Dr Bessel van der Kolk wrote a wonderful book called *The Body Keeps the Score*, in which he describes how traumatic experiences leave traces on minds, emotions, and also on the body. And yes, certain images, feelings, and thoughts related to the past give rise to sensations that can affect the physical body positively or negatively.

Research has shown that images, feelings or thoughts related to love, kindness, joy, peace, happiness, and compassion cause a release of 'happy healing' hormones in the brain such as the endorphins, dopamine, serotonin and melatonin. These 'feel good' brain chemicals can lower blood pressure and heart rate, cholesterol, and heal the body at a cellular level whilst decreasing the shortening of the enzyme – telomeres (a cap-like structure at the ends of each chromosome).

On the other hand, when negative or trauma-related images, feelings or thoughts arise, the Fight-or-Flight response kicks in, and sensations of sweatiness, shortness of breath, increased heart rate, light-headedness, nausea, headaches, and disassociation occur. This causes the chemical cortisol to be released into the brain, and in turn blood platelets become sticky and blood pressure rises. The medium term chain effect of cortisol being released into the brain can lead to weight gain and obesity. Over a prolonged period of time, the negative effects of surplus cortisol on the body can lead to chronic illness like heart disease, cancer or diabetes.

Knowing the basics of the science behind what happens in the body to people with PTSD provides motivation to adopt a mindfulness practice of being in the present moment, on purpose and non-judgementally. This will also help diffuse unnecessary suffering associated with the past.

The anchor of focusing and observing one breath at a time leads a healthy mindfulness practice. The good news here is that as little as three deeper inhales and exhales can immediately activate the parasympathetic nervous system and hack the default mode of the Fight-or-Flight response. This results in a cascading sensation of calmness instantly into the body. It may be a quick fix for that moment, and is better than the alternative.

In practice, mindfulness may not be as easy as it reads on paper to adopt. Persistence is the key to any practice being effective and producing results. But isn't it fascinating to know that something as simple, convenient, and cost-free as breathing in air through the nostrils and into the lungs before exhaling, can alleviate pain and suffering that has arisen due to post-traumatic stress? This simple physical act performed in a conscious state is another friendly reminder that the past does not exist anymore. The only moment that truly exists is this one right now.

Put this handbook down now for a few seconds, take a soft gaze towards your nose tip and reflect on what a relief it is to be able to access a deeper sense calm in the body, activated simply by the breath. As you inhale and exhale, listen to the subtle sound of the air, feel the rising and falling of the chest, and notice your body relaxing.

Now visualise what it would be like to feel your body relaxed and not tensed when negative thoughts, feelings and images arise. An extra dimension to add to focusing on the breath would be to picture any negative thoughts or images as a scene on a movie screen, and on the next exhale of breath, allow the thought or image to dissolve and now enter the gap of 'no thought' before the next scene begins. When practiced regularly and within as little as a few weeks, the brain undergoes a change by forming new neural pathways. This change in the brain is part of neuroplasticity. Studies have shown that people with PTSD who practise this exercise report feeling much less stressed in both mind and body.

Another friendly reminder: the mind works throughout the entire body and not just in the head. The body mirrors the mind and therefore the body keeps the score on what is occurring, moment by moment.

Now: The Present Moment

Key Points

- 'Overthinking' is a modern day affliction
- Being in the present moment can help dissolve painful thoughts of the past
- Practising being present will form a new habit and help you find an alertness and broader sense of awareness

Rob: As you read this book, be mindful of a sense of presence that exists in your hands and feet. Whenever the mind lures you back into the past or far into the future, take a deep breath in and a deep breath out, smile and come back to the present moment. There is nothing more powerful for you than being in the now. In fact, practising being in the present moment can dissolve painful and anxious feelings of the past and the future. There is a deep, calming stillness of consciousness that exists beyond the canvas of the busy, chattering mind. The mind and consciousness are separate from each other.

Unfortunately, many people identify themselves with their mind and the history manifested from past experiences. The mind is not a fan of the present moment and likes to consume consciousness. The past does not exist anymore in reality; it exists only in the mind. So the good news is that when we pay full attention to being present right now and what is going on within our bodies and surroundings, the past and future dissolve.

So right now, practise being present by observing your surroundings in a non-judgemental way and without labelling anything you see. Look up at the sky or something in front of you, feel the texture of the book you are holding, listen to the sounds within your vicinity. Taste any food or drink if it is within reach and be mindful of smells currently existing.

Were you thinking or worrying about anything during this exercise? In this day and age, there seems to be a tendency to overthink things, events, and situations. Although you won't see many documented reports in the media about the modern day addiction called 'thinking'. Yes, of course there is a time to think and plan for continuing to function and live life. Once you have thought about it and know what you need to do, come back to the present moment and rest in a state of being. (Please note this doesn't mean being in a catatonic state or walking around like a zombie!) When practising being present often enough, you will form a new habit and find an alertness and broader sense of awareness arise. And whilst we keep functioning with purpose moment by moment, hour by hour, and day by day, life takes on a new meaning.

As we evolve and continue to live in the now, something amazing occurs. Food tastes better, colours appear brighter, simple things and situations become more interesting, amusing, and delightful. You feel a lightness of being and not so burdened by the past or worried about the future. You also tend to laugh more. Laughter is a great source of natural medicine.

I've heard a number of wounded warriors say that when riding their motorbikes, they feel a sense of freedom, peace, calm, and contentment. It would be safe to say that when you are on a machine with two wheels moving extremely fast, there is no time for distractions other than being attentive to the present moment. And during this experience, people experience longer gaps in between thoughts and images. The thoughts that do arise are not so intense and tend to fade away quickly, evaporated by 'present moment living'.

Another example of people accessing the power of presence is going on a bush walk with family, friends or work colleagues. When there is a close connection with each other in a natural environment where every footstep is different and each tree has its own character and shape, a heightened awareness is present as one delights in the vast variety of plants, animals, and insects anchored by the earth. Sharing the 'moment by moment' experience with others gives rise to collective consciousness. Everyone watches each other's backs, resulting in a strong sense of camaraderie.

Now, stop reading for a few seconds and simply rest in stillness either gently closing the eyes or gazing softly to your nose tip whilst feeling the presence of a subtle energy vibrating through your legs and arms. Now, spend a few moments recalling happy memories. The purpose of this exercise is to demonstrate that not everything from the past needs to be forgotten or suppressed. There is a wonderful saying of Dr Deepak Chopra's along the lines of, "I use the past and don't allow the past to use me."

Because many people in current day society identify themselves with the past whilst placing hope in the future, they find it difficult to live in the present moment. It is enlightening to understand and grasp that the only thing that really exists is this moment, right now. Five minutes from now does not yet exist, and five seconds ago does not exist anymore. When you finally 'get it', a shift in consciousness occurs within the mind to a state of being. At this point, a sense of alertness, awareness, and positive energy kicks in.

Taming the Wild Elephant

Key Points

- Rage, anger or depression can be symbolised by an elephant running wild in your brain
- Mindfulness gives you a number of tools to tame your wild elephant

Rob: Until you accept that the past does not exist anymore and stop identifying with your thoughts and images rather than witnessing them in a non-judgmental fashion, the wild elephant in the mind is likely to trample all over you and everything in its path, causing havoc and destruction. And more than likely, close family and friends will pick up collateral damage.

By always coming back to the next breath in the present moment, feeling and noticing your body, then paying attention to everything related to the inhale and exhale, you have a starting position to tame the wild elephant in the mind. Even if all you ever did was tune into the gentle sound of the breath, eventually the mind helps the elephant to stand still and become tranquil, at least for that moment. You might then consider including another dimension of visualisation. Picture anything that makes you feel calm and peaceful.

The analogy of the elephant – thoughts and images of memories and its association with its tamer – the mind – is fitting. When the mind wallows in the misery of a past event or experience, the elephant becomes increasingly uneasy and starts lumbering off in different directions, causing pain and suffering in the body. And if you keep embellishing the story and scratching the itch of the intrusive thoughts, eventually you lose control of the elephant. It is then that the temptation to ingest medication and/or excessive alcohol surfaces, in order to bring the beast in the mind back into a calm state.

You may say that is easier said than done to tame the wild elephant in the mind by focusing purely on the breathing. However, I have witnessed many PTSD sufferers acting on a leap of faith and trust to begin with, who are now experiencing a life of increased tranquillity without the assistance of artificial substances.

Elephants have long memories and so do human beings, especially if an event was traumatic and stressful. This large animal is also patient, calm, slow-moving, and majestic by nature when treated appropriately. It takes a fair bit of irritation to become angry and upset. In general, humans can be much the same.

So knowing this now, start using tools like the breath to help with the taming process, or simply stretch your arms above your head and look to the sky. In fact, right now, even if you don't feel like it, lift both corners of your mouth and smile for ten seconds. Acknowledge the change in feeling that your body is going through in this moment. If you are having trouble lifting both corners of your mouth, take a pencil, pen or chopstick and place it between both sets of teeth. Studies have shown that this physical action will trigger a release of happy endorphin chemicals in the brain, causing a calming sensation in the body.

Next time something triggers off the memory of a past traumatic event or feelings of anxiety, fear, or depression arise for no apparent reason, I invite you to remember the analogy of the wild elephant and draw on your new skills as its tamer. Before the elephant has a chance to go wild, provide it with reassurance that everything's OK now in this moment by focussing on the details of the next deeper breath. Look up towards the sky or ceiling and feel a sense of presence, awareness, peace, and deeper relaxation.

The following section in this book, Mastering The Mind, invites you to explore a series of exercises to help calm and control your thoughts, taming your own wild elephant.

Mastering the Mind

Whenever you start to experience sensations, images, feelings or thoughts associated with anxiety, anger, depression, frustration or hatred, apply the following methods to help take back control and release the 'happy hormones' of dopamine, serotonin, and melatonin back into the brain.

STOP

Key Points

- S stands for Stop what you are doing
- T stands for Take three deep breaths

- O stands for Observe your body and mind and how you are feeling
- P stands for Proceed with care and compassion to yourself and others in your presence during the moment.

The STOP method is a quick and effective way to diffuse what could potentially become a harmful situation to you, others and anything else within reach.

The trick is being able to recognise when negative or unwanted Sensations, Images, Feelings or Thoughts (SIFT) are about to arise within the mind and body. SIFTing through the situation as best as possible can result in a much better outcome for you and everyone concerned. The more you develop a mindfulness practice, the more sensitive the intelligence of your intuition will become – picking up distress signals from afar before they land in your mind and body.

It is valuable to recognise that when you are fatigued, already irritated or inebriated through the consumption of alcohol or illicit substances, there is an increased probability and frequency of negative SIFT occurring, and at a more rapid rate. Rather than trying to continually avoid smells, sounds, sights, tastes or textures that have previously triggered negative SIFT, be the witness. For example, from a position of pure awareness, watch and notice the SIFT like you are watching a scene from a movie on the screen. Pure awareness (also known as consciousness, spirit, soul) is the observer of the mind and the body. The danger of identifying with SIFT is that they can control and take over your emotions. Be brave and give yourself a chance to understand the difference between your mind and pure awareness. The stillness of this awareness provides a good segue to introduce the STOP methodology as a means to diffuse a potentially harmful situation.

The acronym STOP means exactly what you just read. Stop! When negative sensations, images, feelings, and thoughts arise and the first line of defence – intuition – hasn't been able to stop it at the frontline, then STOP what you are doing, and know that everything's OK now in this present moment. Take three deeper breaths in (you may even like to count to four on the inhale and count to six on the exhale). Ride the waves of each breath (inhale/exhale) like a ship on the ocean, and feel a subtle, calming energy overcome you as it starts to dissolve negative SIFT. It is fascinating that 'the breath' is free, mobile, convenient, immediate and so powerful to help in challenging situations. The 'T' step in the STOP process can take as little as thirty seconds.

Now 'O' is for Observe your body. Acknowledge any negative SIFT and how they are affecting your physical body. This may be expressed as increased heart rate; chilling sensations down the back of the neck; nausea; clenching of teeth and tightness of jaw, eyebrows and other muscles; shortness of breath; light headedness; sweaty hands and other discomforts with which you may be personally familiar.

Feel a transition take place from the Fight-or-Flight response to a more calm and peaceful body and mind. If negative SIFT have not been diffused at this point in time, go back to 'T' and Take three additional, deeper breaths.

'P' completes the process by Proceeding with care and compassion to yourself and others involved in the current situation. This may mean refraining from shouting, rage, violence, self-harm, or verbal abuse, and instead remaining silent, calm, peaceful, patient, and understanding whilst even raising a smile instead of a frown. Know that an act of kindness at this point in time is priceless to everyone concerned in the situation and could potentially prevent an unnecessary event from occurring.

Action Plan

- Right now, take three deep breaths (one breath = inhale/exhale) with a count of four on the inhale and count of six on the exhale
- Acknowledge the different depth of calmness you are experiencing after the three deeper breaths taken
- Reflect on how you would react to a situation after applying the STOP method,

compared to before the reaction having not applied STOP

- Make a real effort to apply STOP each time you start to recognise the beginning of those familiar negative sensations, feelings, images, and thoughts

Spot Reflection

Key Points

- Place small coloured stickers the size of your fingernail on surfaces that you frequently see, e.g. fridge door, back of toilet door, car dashboard, mobile phone cover, bedside table, television
- Each time you notice the coloured stickers, take three deep breaths
- Ride the waves of the three breaths
- Smile for five seconds

Rob: Spot Reflection or Spot Meditation is an effective way of dissolving post-traumatic stress because when one engages the brain in activating the parasympathetic nervous system, new neural pathways start forming in its circuitry. When this occurs on a regular basis for long enough, studies have shown that neuroplasticity occurs. Eventually, the intensity of the negative emotional responses produced during negative sensations, images, feelings, and thoughts (SIFT), begin to lessen, linger, and loop less frequently.

By taking three deeper breaths (inhale/exhale) and intentionally smiling each time you notice your coloured stickers, strategically positioned on everyday objects or surface areas, you create the habit of bringing your brain back into the present moment. With enough practise, whilst activating a calming sensation triggered by the brain's parasympathetic nervous system, the body and mind eventually shift the default mode of Fight-or-Flight to a less negative and intense feeling or sensation when a challenging situation arises.

So what should you reflect on when a small coloured sticker catches your attention during Spot Reflection? You should reflect only on the present moment with each of the three breaths, and how your body and mind are feeling at that time. For example, the coolness of the breath on the inhale and the warmth of the breath on the exhale. The rising and falling of the chest with each breath. Observing a faint, subtle whispering sound of the air entering/exiting the nose; the relaxing of the muscles through the body. Then produce a smile. You can do it: lift both corners of the mouth with those facial muscles. Studies have shown that it actually takes fewer muscles to produce a smile than a frown. If you don't feel like smiling, place a pencil between your top and bottom rows of teeth.

And why is it suggested to place small coloured stickers on surface areas that are viewed regularly? This is so the meditation occurs naturally. Without having to think or remember to take your regular three deeper breaths and smile, it simply becomes incorporated in daily activities. By integrating this easy method into life's essentials, almost no additional effort needs to be applied to access an abundance of calmness on a more regular basis.

Further down the path of this Spot Reflection journey that can be aspired towards lies the eventual result of a highly constant mindful state of being. This occurs when the rising of negative SIFT in the mind, is witnessed by pure awareness, and the processing of that information completely bypasses the amygdala and hippocampus part of the brain (responsible for the Fight-or-Flight reaction), leaving you in the same constant state of peace, calm, and contentment that you were in before, without any negative emotional escalation.

As part of a mindful leadership practice, encourage your loved ones to join in you in this exercise. After all, if they are truly your supporters, they will most probably follow SPOT Reflection as well. It will do everyone the world of good and instil a broader sense of peace and calm among your wider circle of family and friends.

Mind Stillness

Key Points

- Sitting, standing or lying still and mindfully focusing on each natural inhale and exhale of the breath, will eventually quieten the busy and sometimes tormented mind

- It may take a few sessions to become used to this new way of being

Rob: With some determination and persistence, paying attention to the gap of 'nothingness' (also known as field of awareness, inner voice, pure consciousness) that exists in between each thought, will give you the feeling of peace and calmness as the mind takes a rest from being so intrusive towards your real way of being from day to day. Please note, Mind Stillness practice needs to be treated with caution in the event that the person is completely new to this, and has not yet dealt with underlying issues related to traumatic experiences, because it may arouse sensations, images, feelings, and thoughts that have been suppressed for long periods of time.

You are not alone when thinking that your mind cannot stop producing negative thoughts or images. Studies have shown that most people on average have in excess of 60,000 thoughts per day, the largest percentage of these thoughts being negative. And 80% of thinking is unnecessary, meaning that the majority of thinking is related to repetitive thoughts, resentment about past events, and worries about future events.

Social media feeds can also pose a problem. More than ever in today's society, we are surrounded by information – the biggest culprit being the electronic and social media platforms available on handheld devices. Within the last twenty-five years – notably since the widespread adoption of these devices – we have experienced and dealt with more dysfunction, conflict, and neglect than ever before, both as a human race and as a planet. It is not surprising that as a society we are currently facing unprecedented rates of post-traumatic stress, as well as other mental and physical chronic illnesses. Whilst we will never entirely fix all the world's problems, we can start by looking after ourselves.

Because the sky is a blank canvas, it is a great place to look at in order to subside most thoughts and images currently clouding the mind and that no longer serve us. When you overlay the Mind Stillness activity with attention to the breath and everything related to it, you become engulfed with a deeper sense of peace and calm. Over time, you will notice the gaps in between each thought getting longer and longer. It is in these gaps that exists a higher intelligence, healing potential, inner peace, enhanced focus and clarity, answers to questions, and greater intuition.

If you have ever practised meditation exercises before, you might find at first your mind disliking the activity because it is unfamiliar. Your mind may try persistently distracting you back to old habits and usual way of being. When this happens, notice the thought rather than identify with it. In other words, separate yourself from the thought and observe it non-judgementally from your consciousness/field of awareness. Hang in there, persist and soldier on with the breathing techniques. The mind may even try to distract you with hunger pangs and directing your attention to any existing discomfort in your physical body. DON'T GIVE IN TO YOUR MIND. YOU ARE NOT YOUR MIND. You are pure consciousness (the observer of the mind).

This concept may be difficult to grasp straight away. Please have faith and trust that you are not your mind. The past does not exist anymore, the future is unknown, and the only thing that exists is the present moment. Yes, this is all easier said than done. But like other situations in life that may have taken time, belief and patience to achieve an outcome, take a leap of faith and adopt a 'mind stillness' practice long enough to see the results discussed in this chapter.

Wherever I Go, There I Am

Key Points

- You consist of body, mind, and consciousness
- You cannot escape your mind, but you can adapt your thought habits so that negative Sensations, Images, Feelings or Thoughts no longer affect you deeply

Rob: In case you are thinking there must be a safe, healthy way you can escape your mind, then think again! The sooner you accept that wherever you go, your mind follows you, and you commit to applying techniques and methods to deal with its pervasiveness, the sooner you can make peace with yourself. A friendly reminder that the three parts that make you are: Body, Mind, and Consciousness

Yes, by adapting the practice of Mindfulness with simple techniques/tools like STOP, Spot Reflection and remembering to notice any negative SIFT in a non-judgemental way rather identifying with them, you will eventually not care as much that wherever you go, there you are!

Have you ever wondered why many people choose to slip under the canvas of the mind into semi or unconsciousness with excessive alcohol or illicit drugs? More than likely it is to find comfortable numbness away from the pain of the overpowering mind that causes torment. And because the body keeps the score on the mind's pain, unpleasant sensations and feelings appear in many parts of the human anatomy.

Another interesting fact is that many people leave their own home, town or country on vacation to escape their problems. The reality is that travelling to the next town, sailing the seas on a cruise ship, or flying to the other side of the world isn't going to make those problems disappear. Wherever you go physically, your mind containing those problems or 'pain body' goes with you. Yet people subconsciously continue to 'move on' physically, hoping that they are always moving away from the past or future situations they would rather completely forget.

As soon as you accept that 'wherever you go, there you are', and befriend your mind, making peace and agreeing to overcome recurring mental roadblocks and obstacles, a positive life transformation can begin. Because no amount of medication, alcohol or travel will help you to come to terms with your internal war. And as mentioned previously in this book, when you truly realise that you are the witness/observer of your mind and NOT your mind itself, an awakening will occur and a deeper sense of calm and relief is experienced.

In Eckhart Tolle's book, *The Power of Now*, he wrote that as he hit rock bottom, depressed and suicidal, he uttered the words: "I can't live with myself anymore." In that present moment he experienced a major life awakening to the difference between 'I' (pure consciousness/soul/field of awareness) and 'myself' (the mind). Following Eckhart's awakening, peace and serenity followed and ended all the mental torment and suffering that the mind was creating.

Next time a negative sensation, image, feeling or thought surfaces in your mind, notice it by separating yourself from it and observing instead (e.g. as if watching a scene from a movie on TV). As you witness the SIFT, don't put a label on it or entertain it. Acknowledge it and bring your attention immediately to the next few breaths until the unpleasant negative feelings disappear. And each time it recurs, keep bringing your utmost attention back to your breathing. Each of your inhales and exhales are 'present moment' experiences. Note: Sensations and feelings associated with past thoughts and images are NOT the present moment.

Action Plan

- Download the audio book *Wherever You Go, There You Are: Mindfulness Meditation for Everyday Life* by Dr Jon Kabat-Zinn, and listen to it for as many minutes a day as you can spare
- Practice some or all of the techniques suggested in the book
- Make friends with your mind and help it become more peaceful and accepting of any negative sensations, images, feelings or thoughts that may appear throughout the day
- Notice/observe SIFT instead of identifying with them, followed by paying attention to the next breath

Create Real Estate Space in Your Mind

Key Points

- Declutter or 'spring clean' your mind from negative thoughts and images

- The more space there is in the mind, the more peace and tranquillity a person will experience on a day-to-day basis.

Rob: Another way of saying: "I use the past, and don't allow the past to use me" is: "I won't allow any negative thoughts or images to occupy real estate space in my mind". With over 60,000 thoughts crowding the average mind on a daily basis, most of them negative, wouldn't you be motivated to cull the crap, clean out the debris and rubbish, then create real estate space in your mind for something new? Just like the serene feeling of walking through an uncluttered house with plenty of room to manoeuvre, it is equally as peaceful to be free from 'mind congestion'.

In between each thought, there is a gap of 'no thought'. The amount of trauma experienced and the position the reader is on life's journey will have a bearing on the length of the 'no thought' gap. The longer the gaps are of 'no thought' (pure consciousness), the more real estate space exists and expands in the mind. The more real estate space there is in the mind, the more peace and tranquillity a person will experience on a day-to-day basis.

The regular practice of meditation and being mindful is a major enabler to accessing these golden gaps of 'no thought'. The regulation of breathing patterns helps to bring one into a centred, grounded state of being and deeper calm. This in turn can be the doorway to meditation and eventually deeper insight.

Many sufferers of trauma report being reluctant to voluntarily stay still, silent and do nothing for fear of activating flashback memories of traumatic events. People in this situation prefer to keep busy and occupied every minute of the day because subconsciously they know this will limit the probability of unwanted scenarios crowding their mind space. Just like a house requires regular spring-cleaning to keep everything and everyone dust-free and healthy whilst minimising congestion or illness, the mind requires the same. In a house spring-cleaning initiative, many people throw out old furniture, clothes, boxes, and broken items that no longer serve a purpose in the current times. This is a model analogy to draw from for the mind's spring-cleaning exercise.

If you are prepared to clean up your house, why would you not apply some simple techniques to expand the mind's real estate space and unclutter it from the mental torment that does not serve it anymore?

Keep the process simple. Just have faith and trust, and create a new habit of doing the basic steps suggested.

Action Plan

- Each time a thought arises in your mind, notice it (don't identify with it), and make an assessment whether it will benefit you or not
- Ask the question: "Do I really want that negative image or thought renting real estate space in my head?" If the answer is no, consciously exhale it out of your mind with the next breath

- Find ten minutes each day to sit comfortably somewhere quiet and repeat to yourself on each breath inhale: "Create new mind space" and on each exhale, repeat to yourself: "Empty the crap"

Harmonic Sound Vibrations a.k.a. Music

Key Points

- Music can directly influence the amount of cortisol (stress hormone) released from the brain
- Music can be a powerful part of the Mindfulness process

Rob: For thousands of years the harmonic sound vibrations of music has been listened to and used as a way to heal, and create peace and harmony amongst individuals and groups all over the planet. And when you overlay song lyrics over the sounds, you are privy to another dimension of meaning and mood-enhancing wellness for the mind, body, and soul. Thanks to technology, never before has it been more convenient to access on demand music of your choice.

Experts have scientifically proven that many specific clusters of sounds or song pieces further enhance the healing process of the mind. Sometimes it is as simple as the rhythmic tapping of fingers on a cardboard box; sometime as complex as the coordinated sounds from all the instruments in a full orchestra. And anywhere in between it could be the harmonised voices of an a capella singing group, jazz, or heavy rock and roll band. For many reasons in both a scientific and spiritual sense, the harmonic sound vibrations of music resonate at a cellular level within the human body and mind, in most cases creating a calmer and more peaceful state of being. Studies have shown that listening to certain types of music can have benefits including lower blood pressure, reduced anxiety, uplifted moods, decreased levels of the stress hormone cortisol, better sleep, reduced depression, strengthened memory and learning ability, reduced pain, and a healthy brain.

Other symptoms in the body and mind that are associated with the positive effects of harmonic vibrations and music include relaxed muscles, slower breathing patterns, smiles and laughter, and a general feeling of wellbeing throughout the body.

Studies have shown that in particular, slow, quiet classical music and guitar have even greater calming effects on the mind and body by decreasing the levels of cortisol. Findings indicate that first responders and soldiers that have undergone long-term stress are susceptible to illness due to their immune systems being compromised by cortisol.

Suggested effective ways to listen to music and enjoy the harmonics of sound is by either sitting comfortably in a quiet, non-distracting environment, whilst practicing warrior body movements, going for a walk or jog, cooking, or driving, just to name a few.

Action Plan

- Choose music pieces or songs you feel will relax and make you calm
- Find a quiet place to listen to your music – this can be done either in stillness or in motion
- Listen and absorb the harmonic vibrations of sound and be attentive to how it makes your body and mind feel

Smile and Laugh Out Loud!

Key Points:

Rob: Even when you don't feel like smiling and/or laughing out loud, when you do, studies have shown that powerful, healing 'feel good' chemicals like serotonin, melatonin, and dopamine are released into the brain, causing the mind and body to dissolve any lingering stress. And, as I said earlier, it actually takes fewer facial muscles to activate a smile than it does to frown. So really it comes down to making the choice to smile or frown. It may prove challenging for some of us to laugh and smile whenever we feel like it due to old belief systems that as adults or as warriors, we are supposed to be serious, frown, and hide our feelings.

Can you recall a funny movie or comedy show you've watched any time in your lifetime? Now can you recall a particular scene in that movie that made you laugh uncontrollably? If so, you might be on the verge of at least raising a smile! If not, I suggest you find out what is available online to download and watch to give you this healing and euphoric feeling of bliss and joy. Not only will your body's biological cells benefit from the laughter, the mind may take a break from any recurring loops of traumatic memories or situations.

Laughter yoga is another great way to evolve a smile and constant chuckling for a while. If you cannot find a laughter yoga class in your area, search it on YouTube and get a taste that way. Because laughter is contagious, all it takes is for one person to start laughing uncontrollably out loud even if it is forced and doesn't arise naturally. Even if someone starts 'fake laughing', e.g. HA HA HA HA HA for long enough, it can eventually cause others to start a genuine laugh. For many people, witnessing laughter or smiles cause the act to spread like a virus. Before you know it, tears of joy are running unbidden down people's cheeks.

As previously discussed, thanks to the latest brain scan technology, it is possible to prove the release of natural chemicals into the brain in response to certain thought patterns or emotions. The brain has its own pharmacy of chemicals – some good, some not so good. Studies have shown that a number of these chemicals secreted by the brain contain natural healing properties for the mind and body.

I dare you to start laughing out loud now. If you are in a public area and are worried about what others within earshot might think of you, go to a place where you cannot be seen or heard and start laughing. At this point if this is too challenging, smile instead.

Action Plan

- Right now, lift both corners of your mouth and smile ☺
- If you are having difficulty smiling unaided, then get a pencil, pen, spoon or chopstick and place it horizontally between your teeth, gently holding it in place
- Hold this position for thirty seconds and notice how your body changes as the 'feel good' chemicals released in the brain cascade down into parts of the body
- On a daily basis, 'use the past' to think of something funny. Now laugh out loud!
- Make a conscious effort to smile (even if it's just to yourself) for five seconds every couple of hours between waking up and going to bed until it becomes second nature and a new way of being.

Deploying the Body

The Importance of Exercise

Key Points

- Keep physically fit. It doesn't matter what you do: just do something!
- Establish a routine and make exercise a priority
- A healthy body equals a healthy mind
- Yoga and Pilates are excellent forms of exercise that get you out of the house and calm the mind while you are exercising

Todd: Military organisations all over the globe invest a lot of time and money getting their entry-level members physically fit. It is, of course, the same for first responders. While a candidate or recruit is increasing their personal level of physical fitness, the mental pressure associated with being indoctrinated into an alien environment coupled with learning the basic skills of a military force is notably reduced.

My first few days at the Recruit Training Battalion at Kapooka in NSW passed at one hundred miles an hour. Our feet did not touch the ground; it was a whirlwind of demands, orders, and our introduction to the Army training system. Every minute of every day was accounted for, and the only time we had to ourselves was when our heads hit the pillow at night. I was physically tired and mentally drained at the end of every day; there was not much time to myself as it was literally lights out. Until I was aroused by 'hallway four', where each recruit bounded out of bed with one sheet over his shoulder to stand to attention in the hallway.

The physical system in which we were now indoctrinated included running, circuits, swimming, and route marches. My platoon, along with a few others, was involved in weight load trials. Our sister platoon undertook the extant physical training system, whereas our platoon walked everywhere with our packs on. Of course there was not much running, which I initially thought was a godsend. Over time our packs got heavier and heavier and the distances we walked increased significantly. Unfortunately for us, our sister platoon absolutely smashed us in all of the benchmark physical assessments, including the route marches. In fact many of us, myself included, actually put on weight during our time in recruit training, which of course was not ideal.

The negative impact of this did not come to light until those of us 'selected' for infantry training arrived at the School of Infantry at Singleton, NSW. Being behind the eight ball at the start of the physically demanding four-month infantry training was less than idyllic. Many of us were constantly exhausted and therefore struggled with the theory and academic aspects of being a grunt. I did not bridge the gap of being a fitness minnow until I marched into an Infantry Battalion, where I had spare time to work on my fitness outside of business hours. I was also fortunate enough to have new mates who assisted me to get back into condition.

Using myself as a case study, I have found over the years that when I am physically fit and strong I am in a much better position to combat psychopathology. The old adage mentioned throughout this book – healthy body equals a healthy mind – certainly rings true. Not quite in the sense of the statement's intent, but I am certainly in a stronger frame of mind and my resilience to obstacles and difficulties is much better. I am not stating that being physically fit removes your troubles but I do believe that it does dilute them.

As I wrote in *Dissolving Past Traumatic Stress Part I*, in August 2014 I travelled to Borneo to trek the Sandakan Death March with other men and women who have been affected by their service to Australia. I was extremely unfit at the time and approximately 30kg overweight, although I didn't realise it until afterwards, when I saw some of the photos of myself that were taken on the trip. Oh my God! I was absolutely huge – no wonder I found all of those steep ascents in the humid jungle so difficult. Upon my return, I started to train regularly and I also paid better attention to my diet.

In my younger years I used to be of the mindset that if I wasn't running ten kilometres it was a waste of time. My philosophy now is 'just do something'. About a month after our return I was invited to speak at a corporate event. I had lost about 10kg at this stage and I was feeling pretty good about myself. It was at this event that I met Paul de Gelder, the former grunt and Navy clearance diver I wrote about previously who was attacked by a bull shark in Sydney Harbour. I had read his book and was absolutely amazed by his presentation. Now, this guy is incredibly fit. I thought to myself at the time, *If someone with one arm and one leg can be incredibly fit, then, Toddo, you have no excuse.* At the completion of his presentation, Paul said something that resonated with me: "If I have shamed you into getting fit, then good." Yep, Paul, you shamed me but I am so glad that you did.

Immediately I set myself a goal of completing a half-ironman triathlon. Why a triathlon? Because I swim like a set of car keys, I am terrible on the bike, and I'm a poor runner so it just made sense. I developed a training program and stuck to it. For once I felt completely in control of my life and I took pride in my increasing fitness and decreasing waistline. It was an amazing feeling when I crossed that finish line. It was ridiculously hot – 37°C – but I had heaps of support. I wore my Soldier On cycling top and everyone along the course cheered on the fat blokes! I think there were three of us.

With the completion of my triathlon, fitness was ticked off my list but I now had to work on my weight. It has been a struggle as I naturally have a slow metabolism and all the medication I am on is designed to slow me down further. Even when I was in the Army and at times was very fit, I just didn't look it. No excuses, though. It took a further three months to get below 100kg, with my ultimate goal being 90kg. I am now sitting at 88kg and I'm really happy with that. I have also found that as I am training for the New York Marathon this year, being lighter makes it easier to run – go figure.

Warrior Body Movement

Key Points

- This next section of the book introduces a series of yoga poses we shall call Warrior Body Movement
- In conjunction with a healthy Mindfulness practice, yoga can benefit the body in many ways by increasing blood flow, toning the muscles, increasing flexibility, and instilling a deeper sense of calm
- Just ten minutes per day can have dramatic and beneficial effects

Rob: Moving your body slowly and stretching it out gently in different directions and angles with the mindset of a peaceful but powerful warrior, will create a sense of relaxation, calm, and freedom among the muscles, joints, tendons, ligaments, and bones. It also helps connect the dots between the mind and the body, as the two are connected. A calm mind is a calm body and vice versa. Every corresponding knot in the body has a corresponding knot in the mind. This exercise can be performed anywhere from as little as ten minutes per day to start reaping immediate benefits.

At any time through the practice of these warrior body movements, it is important to listen to your body and not push the limit. An indication that you have pushed your body over the limit can express itself as sharp, sudden pains or holding the breath.

Move into each position softly and slowly. The human body mostly consists of fluid, so flow like water and soften like air with each movement. Start to develop an awareness of the link between the mind and the body. Be present too, and feel what is happening in each and every part of the body throughout the duration of movements. As you create freedom in the body by gently stretching and extending the muscles in different angles, the mind responds in a positive way.

Warrior I

- Place one foot forward, one foot back whilst facing the front
- Inhale, raise the arms up parallel to each other, looking up in between the hands
- Exhale whilst leaning into the bent knee and leg of the front foot

- Hold for five breaths
- Swap legs and perform Warrior I on the opposite side

Warrior II

- Place both feet one-and-a-half leg lengths apart
- Extend both arms horizontal to the floor
- Turn the head to gaze softly beyond the front-facing hand

- Exhale and bend the knee of the front leg
- Hold for five breaths
- Swap sides and perform Warrior II on the opposite side

Warrior III

- Facing forward, come to a balancing position on one leg
- Hinging forward at the hips, straighten the other leg lifted parallel to the ground
- Reach forward with straight arms out front, parallel to each other and the ground

- Look in between the hands and take three breaths
- Repeat Warrior III on the other leg

Reverse Warrior

- Refer to the instructions of the Warrior II position and take that stance

- Inhale as you raise your front-facing arm up and over your head, while your eye view follows the rising hand
- Exhale and slide the other hand down the back straightened leg
- Take three breaths and swap sides

Humble Warrior

- Start in a kneeling position with knees wider than hip width
- Extend the buttocks back towards the heels
- Exhale and reach forward with both arms parallel and hands on the floor

- Forehead makes contact with the floor
- Take ten breaths and relax the jaw and every muscle in the body

Upward-facing Warrior

- Lie face down on the floor
- Inhale and bring both hands to each side of the chest with elbows bent
- Extend arms straight and arch the back, looking up towards the ceiling beyond your eyebrow centre (optional: lift knees off the floor)
- Take three-to-five breaths

Downward-facing Warrior

- From a kneeling position, place hands on the floor, fingers spread wide, shoulders and arms stacked on top of the hands
- Lift knees off the floor, straighten legs
- Exhale and track the chest back towards the thighs (looking at the feet, calf or thigh muscles)
- Assume the position of a triangle (with buttocks at the apex and hands and feet planted firmly on the floor)
- Take five-to-seven breaths

Warrior Rising

- Stand to attention with quadriceps activated, the pit of the belly drawn in towards the spine, shoulders rolled back, and neck lengthened with chin slightly tucked in towards chest

- Inhale and raise both arms up in parallel towards the ceiling or sky
- Take five breaths (with each inhale reach up further, trying to touch the ceiling/sky) and feel the lengthening of the muscles up and down both sides of the body.

Resting Warrior

- Lie down flat on your back with your eyes closed or a soft gaze up towards the ceiling/sky
- Allow your feet to fall out to the sides and relax your hands (palms facing upwards)

- Exhale deeply and allow the floor to take all the weight of your body
- Completely let go and relax whilst surfing the waves of each breath for at least five minutes

Beyond the Four Fs

Key Points:

- Humans have evolved to have four basic drives: Fighting, Fleeing, Feeding and Reproducing
- In times of stress the body resorts to these four emotional responses
- It is possible to overcome these urges with a combination of breathing exercises, mindfulness, warrior body movements, and communication

Rob: Approximately 300 million years ago, the reptilian part of the brain evolved among human beings. This contains the 'command control centre' responsible for the Four Fs: Fighting, Fleeing, Feeding and Reproducing. It is basic human instinct to run away from danger, confront and protect what is yours, eat when hungry, and procreate to expand the family whilst satisfying sexual urges. History suggests that humans default towards these instinctual behaviours, especially in time of survival.

Common sensations to recognise with each of the Four Fs:

- Fighting: an increase in heart rate; tension in jaw; clenching of teeth; faster, more shallow breathing; clenching of fists; stronger heartbeats; sweating; flaring of nostrils.
- Fleeing: eyelids widen; sweating; increased heart rate; shortness of breath; stronger heartbeats; looking for escape exits; nausea; incontinence
- Feeding: hunger pangs; salivation; visualisation of favourite food
- Reproducing: arousal in the reproductive organs; increased heart rate; sweatiness; deeper breathing

These feelings naturally come and go and you may have noticed that they linger for longer and sometimes shorter periods of time, depending on what you are doing in the moment. It could be that you force yourself to be distracted by finding something new to do in order to forget one of the Four Fs being experienced.

Set yourself the challenge to move beyond the Four Fs – especially the first two, Fighting and Fleeing – when an uncomfortable situation arises. Performing a few warrior body movements, breathing exercises and being non-judgemental towards the situation can successfully achieve this.

To diffuse a potentially regretful and harmful situation – e.g. loss of temper/rage, physical or mental violence, forced sexual act without consent, overeating, unnecessary sudden increase in blood pressure, and any other action that you may have experienced by letting one or all of the Four Fs control you – refocus your attention by using some or all of the following tips:

- Ride the waves of deeper breaths in and out through the nostrils
- Splash your face with cold water

- Look up and gaze at the sky
- Make contact with a family member, friend or supporter and thank them for caring about you
- Play or listen to relaxing music on your handheld device (YouTube's sounds of nature, harp, piano)
- Perform warrior body movement exercises
- Fix your gaze on one thing in particular and observe all the finer details associated with the object

Do not give in to the power of the mind by scratching the itch and engaging the thought created by an F feeling. Be encouraged to know that by returning to the most basic life force of all – the breath – that the unwanted feeling will eventually subside and return you to a more evolved conscious state of being.

Action Plan

- Unless it is dinnertime or an opportunity to display love towards your partner, move beyond the Four Fs by focusing on one inhale and exhale at a time until the sensations, images, thoughts or feelings pass you by

- Engage yourself in a few warrior body movements until the Four Fs subside
- Look up at the sky until the urge to engage the Four Fs subsides.

A Conscious Diet

Key Points

- Food is medicine, conversely it is poison
- Eat clean and natural foods
- Food high in sugar and carbohydrates will affect your mood

Rob: Have you ever heard the saying: "You are what you eat?" My response to this is, "If it swims or grows in the ground, eat it!" There are many foods that can dissolve stress when consumed often enough. Fish like salmon, tuna, and snapper when grilled, baked or steamed, with a serving of fresh vegetables eaten on a regular basis, can invoke a feeling of wellbeing, and stabilise and minimise mood swings, just to name a few health benefits. Finish the meal off with a square or two of good quality dark chocolate and feel the mood-enhancing cocoa do the work to give you an added sense of euphoria. Now, chocolate doesn't grow in the ground, however the cocoa beans it originates from do.

And before you think about teaching a pig, chicken, sheep or cow to swim, think again. These animals are not the food types we are referring to here. Studies have shown that taking the option to eat fish is better for cholesterol levels and blood pressure control than any white or red meats. Having said that, a much harder choice is to become a vegetarian. Research has also shown that a vegetarian diet can even further enhance mind and body wellness.

When certain foods can affect moods and one is suffering from post-traumatic stress, it makes sense to minimise mental and physical irritation and maximise calmness in the mind. The mind exists in every cell of the physical body, not just in the head.

In the event you are looking for a new hobby that also promotes a mindfulness practice, consider starting a vegetable garden, planting seedlings, and growing your own fresh, organic, vitamin-rich food. The additional vitamins, minerals and goodness that come from home-grown vegetables are wonderful for the healing process.

Another hobby to consider is fishing. And yes, studies have also shown that wild fish have more nutrients than farmed fish. Although returning to the days of hunter/gatherer may be contrary to the modern lifestyle many are accustomed to, it is certainly worth considering as an activity to help dissolve stress.

In the meantime, head down to the local supermarket or fresh food market and buy some fish and vegetables for lunch or dinner. Either by yourself or with loved ones, go online and find a new recipe to follow before cooking up and mindfully munching nutritious substances from the ground and water.

Action Plan

- Eat some fish and vegetables tonight for dinner
- Avoid or eat less red meat and incorporate at least two servings of grilled or steamed fish per week, plus daily servings of fresh, brightly coloured vegetables
- Invest in a quality block of dark chocolate with at least 70% cocoa content and mindfully eat a couple of squares daily. Notice the aroma, flavour, and texture of this mood-enhancing food.

And So To Bed

Key Points

- When the body is sufficiently rested, the mind is also in a much better state
- Recent studies have shown that six to eight hours of deep sleep per night is optimal for wellbeing

Rob: The health benefits of good sleep are well known, and recent studies have shown that six to eight hours of deep sleep per night are optimal for wellbeing. This state of consciousness assists the body at a cellular level to return to homeostasis (a perfect biological balance within the body). When the body is sufficiently well rested, the mind is also in a much better state and will experience less irritability, negative thoughts, anxiety or depression.

When the body and mind are in a state of deep rest for long enough, healing of inflammation and dysfunction occurs. As to what quantified levels, we are still unsure exactly. Continual research and focused attention to the area of sleep is being conducted. Reporting enhanced feelings of rejuvenation after a good night's sleep is common feedback, indicating that when one is in a state of deep rest for a long enough period, the body's naturally produced 'feel good' hormones, dopamine, serotonin, and melatonin, have a chance to work their magic. On the opposite end of the scale, when the body is deprived of sleep, the stress hormone, cortisol, is overly produced and results in causing a rise in blood pressure, uneasiness, an increased appetite, irritability, and mood swings. And with PTSD regularly affecting quality of sleep (without the use of drugs), the deprivation of this wonderful resting habit can easily trigger negative sensations, images, feelings and thoughts.

It actually becomes easier to sleep deeper and longer in general when many of the other suggested wellness models in this book are practised on a daily basis. There is a correlation between good sleep patterns, diet, exercise, mindfulness, and positive outlooks on life.

The other popular current sleep recommendation involves 'power naps' or mini sleeps during the mid afternoon. This new habit need not last any longer than between ten and forty-five minutes. If you are not at home or in the vicinity of a bed, be creative and sit in the car with the seat reclined or rest on a park bench, in an office chair or on a yoga mat. It has been said that a short nap in the afternoon each day can result in a longer lifespan, not to mention, a boost of energy for the rest of the day plus an uplift in mood.

Try and avoid a warmer climate during sleep time. The body will find it easier to stay settled when the temperature is slightly cooler, e.g. 18-22°C.

And if you are having trouble getting to sleep either for the night or just a power nap, focus on the sound and feeling of each breath as you inhale and exhale. The other method to consider practising is to count down from ninety-nine with each breath.

Action Plan

- Before retiring for the evening, ensure that you have not eaten anything for approximately two hours, and turn off your mobile phone, radio, and TV
- Keep the bedroom quiet even if it means closing the window, and maximise the darkness with heavy curtains or blinds (if possible)

- As you lie with your head on the pillow, take ten deeper breaths (counting to eight on the inhale and exhale), while replaying the day's events. Let go of each event on the exhale. This helps to clear space in the mind and make you more tranquil.
- Acknowledge the new calmness your body feels now. Close your eyes and drift off to sleep.

Epilogue

With the PTSD epidemic modern society is facing today, we feel it is our duty of service to raise awareness, and provide insight and tools in an accessible and easy to understand way that will assist people living with the condition to suffer less, improve quality of life, and get on with living more peacefully, joyfully, and harmoniously.

Now that you have had insight from this handbook into proven methods that can dissolve post-traumatic stress, it might be a good time to go back through the various chapters and highlight or place a marker on phrases or pages that resonated with you. This could then be viewed as your own customised toolkit to refer to when faced with a challenge related to PTSD.

If there were any pages of the book you could not relate to, that's OK. It could mean you weren't ready to hear that information at the time. Rereading *Everything's OK: Past Traumatic Stress Dissolved* at different stages during your recovery will be helpful to reinforce messages and discover new insight that may not have been absorbed in the mind the first time.

Feel free to also pass on this book or recommend it to someone else you know who could use the help it offers.

Contact your local veteran support organisation for further assistance.

Thank you for taking the time to read this book. We wish you the very best in your recovery.

Todd Berry & Rob Ginnivan
August 2017

Acknowledgements

A big thank you goes to all the people who have served their country in an endeavour to protect the community. In particular, we thank and acknowledge those wounded warriors for the good deeds they have done for society whilst in the process being affected and injured. Our deepest gratitude goes to the leaders that have inspired and imparted wisdom upon us over time to help make this book a vehicle to assist those living with PTSD and their family and friends to feel better and become well again. And a great appreciation for our loved ones, who continue to support us on this challenging journey.

Todd: I would like to thank my wonderful wife, Suzy, for her love and support. She has changed me from existing to living.

Rob: Thank you to my creatively gifted daughter, Annika Ginnivan, who captures the essence of mindful body movement in the book's photos.

Notes

Notes

Notes

Notes

Notes

Notes

Printed in the United States
By Bookmasters